Cooking
on the Road
WITH CELEBRITY CHEFS

Publisher: Joe Daquino
Associate Publisher: Ann Emerson
Project Manager: Genevieve Branco
Production Team: Gary Guthrie, Alyssa Halberg
Editor: Anne de Ravel
Layout: Sarah Rainwater
Cover Design: Sarah Rainwater
Cover Photographs: (top) © Melanie Acevedo, Food Pix, Jupiter Images
                   (bottom) © Eastcott Momatiuk, The Image Bank, Getty Images

Printed and bound in the United States by Ripon Printers.
Bookstore distribution by The Globe Pequot Press.

For more information about Woodall's products and services go to: www.woodalls.com
or call 1-800-323-9076.

ISBN 10: 0-912082-08-9
ISBN 13: 978-0-912082-08-0

Foreword
Anne de Ravel

While the thrill and excitement of a RV camping trip is about relaxing and enjoying the beauty of natural surroundings, once upon a time, this yearning for discovery and freedom also entailed trading great home cooking for mediocre meals. Baked beans from the can, sorry-looking produce, and stale bread and hot dog rolls were more than just an option—they were the reality.

We've come a long way from those dreary days! Today when it comes to dining out, home cooking, recipes and ingredients, we have become a sophisticated nation curious to explore new cuisines and flavors. And when leaving the comfort of our homes, we no longer need to compromise.

RV galleys have become more cook friendly and conducive to interesting wholesome cookery. Outfitted with subzero refrigerators, state-of-the art ranges and ovens, better equipment and clever storage space, they are designed for ease and efficiency and, of course, great cooking. Thanks to internet access, we can now purchase the most unusual ingredients or locate interesting local food markets while on the road—and the GPS technology can take us there! Supermarkets around the country have become more enticing, often offering better produce and a wide range of ingredients and condiments. And lately, campgrounds are slowly stepping up to the trend with onsite stores carrying quality products such as F. Ottomanelli's CAMPOTTO.COM, a selection of top quality meats especially packaged for RVers and campers.

left: galley of
Country Coach's
luxurious Affinity
Custom RV.

right: **Winnebago's**
stylish Adventurer.

Cooking on the Road with Celebrity Chefs is a collection of recipes from some of the most talented chefs in this country. Ranging from contemporary flavors to updated regional classics, the recipes reflect this innovative movement toward greater diversity and creativity when it comes to food. Thumbing through the book you'll meet our culinary experts, learn about their unique personalities and style in the kitchen and on the road, their approach to easy camp dining without sacrificing flavors or quality, how they cope with limited equipment at their disposal and some of their favorite destinations.

From TV personality Chef Harry, who cruises this country's supermarkets with the curiosity of an anthropologist, to rising star Melissa Perello, executive chef at the Fifth Floor Restaurant in San Francisco, who favors solo hikes in the California outback, you'll peek into their lives and learn some great tricks of the trade along the way. The recipe collection is geared to a broad range of cooking skills, culinary interests and discerning palates from easy aromatic spice rubs and salsas, inspired burgers, deep-flavored stews, and robust breakfast grub to more exotic fare such as lemongrass butternut squash soup—there is something for everyone and for every meal of the day. You will also find useful tips on packing and preparing ahead of time. And because spontaneity and resourcefulness are the signs of a great chef, you'll also find suggestions on substituting and adapting a recipe based on what is in your galley and your location.

Whether you are cruising this country's highways as full time RVers or for short vacations and weekends, we think you'll find this book engaging and most delicious.

Campground

1

Eggs in a Hole

GUY MICHAUD

This recipe is a perennial favorite with children. For a grown-up touch, add a dash of your favorite hot sauce and/or a sprinkling of minced fresh herbs such as chives, tarragon, basil or any combination just before serving.

TWO SERVINGS

2 thick slices of good quality white
   or whole wheat bread
3 tablespoons butter
2 large eggs
Salt and freshly ground pepper to
   taste

2 tablespoons grated Fontina,
   Gruyere or Manchego cheese,
   or more to taste

Make a 1 ½ to 2-inch hole at the center of each slice of bread.

Heat the butter in a small frying pan over medium-high heat. Add the bread slices to the pan and cook for about 2 minutes on each side to coat with butter and lightly toast them. Lower the heat to medium and carefully crack an egg into each hole. Cook for about 2 minutes to set the eggs. Carefully flip the toasts with a flat spatula and sprinkle with the grated cheese. Cook until the eggs are cooked to the desired consistency and the cheese is melted, about 2 minutes for runny yolks.

Eggs and Chorizo Frittata

GUY MICHAUD

A hearty satisfying breakfast, this frittata is also terrific when tucked into a crusty roll with ripe tomato slices and spicy greens such as arugula or watercress.

FOUR SERVINGS

1 tablespoon olive oil
⅓ cup thinly sliced Spanish chorizo
    sausage or your favorite spicy
    cured sausage (see note)
1 small onion, thinly sliced
2 garlic cloves, minced

3 to 4 thin slices Cheddar or
    Manchego cheese
4 basil leaves, thinly sliced
8 large eggs, beaten
Homemade or store-bought tomato
    salsa

Note: Chorizo is a cured spicy sausage from Spain. It is available in most supermarkets or can be purchased online. See resource page 202.

Preheat the oven to 400° F.

Heat the olive oil in a nonstick oven-proof pan over medium heat. Add the chorizo or spicy sausage and sauté until lightly browned on both sides. Add the onion and garlic and cook until the onion is soft and translucent. Season with salt and pepper to taste.

Spread the sausage and onion mixture and layer the cheese slices on top. Sprinkle with the basil. Pour the eggs over the layers and place the pan in the oven. Bake for 5 to 8 minutes, until the eggs are just set. Do not overcook. Remove from the oven and let the frittata settle for 5 minutes.

Run a rubber spatula around the inside edge of the pan and invert the frittata onto a serving plate. Cut into wedges and serve with tomato salsa. The frittata can be served hot or at room temperature.

Chorizo Scramble

NEAL FRASER

Although this big flavor breakfast doesn't need too many other fixings, a spoonful or two of refried beans and warm tortillas would round out this meal pretty nicely.

SIX SERVINGS

3 tablespoons olive oil
3 fingerling potatoes, thinly sliced
½ cup thinly sliced Spanish chorizo
    (see note)
10 roasted piquillo peppers, cut into
    thin strips (see note)

12 large eggs, beaten
¼ cup grated Manchego or Parmesan
    cheese
½ teaspoon smoked paprika
Salt to taste

Note: Piquillo peppers are slightly spicy peppers from Spain. They are available in jars or cans in specialty gourmet stores and upscale supermarkets, or can be purchased online. Chorizo is a cured spicy sausage from Spain. It is available in most supermarkets or can be purchased online. See resource page 202.

Heat the oil in a nonstick sauté pan over medium-high heat. Add the sliced potatoes and cook, stirring once in a while, until soft, about 5 minutes.

Add the sliced chorizo to the pan and cook, stirring, for 4 minutes. Add the peppers and cook for another minute or until hot. Lower the heat to medium.

Pour in the beaten eggs and sprinkle with the Manchego or Parmesan cheese. Cook, stirring constantly, until the eggs are set but still soft. Sprinkle with salt and smoked paprika and serve immediately.

Crisp and Light Rice Flour Waffles

JAMIE RORABACK

Homemade waffles are delicious breakfast treats. The addition of rice flour gives these a pleasing crispness. They can be prepared ahead of time and kept frozen. Just pop them in a toaster when ready to serve.

FOUR SERVINGS

½ cup all-purpose flour
½ cup rice flour, available in supermarkets in Asian or Latin section
¼ teaspoon salt

1 ½ teaspoons baking powder
2 large eggs, separated
¾ cup milk
4 tablespoons butter, melted
1 tablespoon sugar

Preheat the waffle iron.

Sift together the flour, rice flour, salt and baking powder into a large bowl. In a separate bowl, whisk together the 2 egg yolks, milk and melted butter. Pour the liquid mixture into the dry ingredients and stir until just combined.

In a separate bowl, whip the 2 egg whites to a soft peak; add the sugar and whip until stiff and shiny. Fold the egg whites into the batter.

Lightly grease the preheated waffle iron and pour enough batter to almost cover the surface. Close the iron. Cook the waffles until deep golden and crisp. Serve warm with your favorite toppings.

Chef
Jamie Roraback

CHEF/INSTRUCTOR,
Connecticut Culinary Institute

Studio or Campsite Cooking

This fearless chef just completed his first 500 cooking segments on Connecticut's local NBC station without any single cut or burn! He is also the host of *Cooking from the Campsite with Chef Jamie*, a 13-part series taped on location in Vermont showcasing local produce and outdoor cooking.

Fire Up the Grill!

A graduate of the CIA (Culinary Institute of America) in Hyde Park, New York, Chef Jamie is impeccably trained in the finest techniques and disciplines of the culinary arts. But once he hangs up his chef's jacket, you will most likely find Jamie having fun tending the grill and creating casual outdoor feasts for family and friends.

Showmanship

Jamie has an infectious enthusiasm for outdoor cooking, "You cook better, and it's not messy." Plus, he says, when you're in a wide-open space, you can flambé and let the flames shoot sky high. But less experienced outdoor cooks, don't try this at home—or your campsite!

A Father's Legacy

Jamie credits his father for his unconditional love of cooking on an open fire. His dad, who wasn't a professional chef, prepared most of the family meals, from fish to Spam, in a skillet set in their home fireplace in Middlefield, CT.

First Cooking Accolade

Jamie received his only Boy Scout merit badge for—you guessed it—cooking. Although the chef doesn't remember what he prepared, he is certain that chicken and dumplings simmered in a Dutch oven were on the menu. "They were very fashionable at the time," says Roraback.

Most Memorable Camping Experience

During one of his live segments on camp cooking, unbeknownst to his show producers, Jamie proposed to his (then) girlfriend Alison. A little startled but undeterred, the young lady took the ring. They have been camping happily ever after.

Favorite Destination as a Chef

He adores Vermont for its infinite array of organic farm stands, artisanal bread and cheese makers, smokehouses, microbreweries, superb maple syrup and fruit wineries.

Best Advice to the Outdoor Cook

It's similar to what he instills in his professional students: Do all your *mise en place* (prepping) before you start cooking. It is one of the essential skills needed to become a successful outdoor chef—or any chef, for that matter. "Every ingredient has to be cut, peeled and ready to go. Once you start cooking, everything happens very quickly; you can easily lose track of what is going on."

Breakfast Blintzes with Lemon Cheese Filling and Blueberry Syrup

JAMIE RORABACK

Save this recipe for rainy days. It is more involved than the average breakfast fare and should be savored at leisure.

MAKES ABOUT 10 BLINTZES

BATTER:
2 large eggs
1 cup milk
4 tablespoons butter, melted
1 cup all-purpose flour
1 pinch salt
Vegetable oil spray as needed

FILLING:
1 ½ cups ricotta cheese
1 ½ cups cream cheese, softened
2 tablespoons finely grated lemon zest
2 cups frozen blueberries
¾ cup light corn syrup
2 tablespoons lemon juice
Whipped cream, ice cream and powdered sugar for garnish (optional)

To make the batter: whisk together the eggs, milk and butter in a mixing bowl. Sift together the flour and salt over the mixture and whisk until just combined. Do not over beat. Cover the bowl and refrigerate for at least 30 minutes or overnight.

Heat an 8-inch nonstick pan over medium heat and lightly coat with some vegetable oil spray. Pour about 2 tablespoons batter into the pan and immediately swirl to coat the bottom evenly. Cook until the crepe batter sets and the bottom is lightly browned, about 2 minutes. Loosen the crepe and flip it with a thin spatula. Cook on the other side for about 1 minute. Slide the crepe onto a plate and repeat until all the batter has been used. Cover the stack of crepes as you go along with a towel to keep them from drying out.

Combine the ricotta cheese, cream cheese and lemon zest in a mixing bowl until smooth.

In a small saucepan, combine the blueberries, corn syrup and lemon juice. Bring to a simmer over medium heat. Remove from the heat.

When ready to serve, place the crepes on a work surface, spoon an equal amount of the filling at the center of each one and shape into a cylinder. Fold the sides over the filling and roll into a flat cylinder.

Serve immediately with the warm blueberry syrup. As an alternative, the blintzes can be gently sautéed in a little butter to warm the filling and lightly brown them before topping with the syrup. Garnish with whipped cream, ice cream or powdered sugar (optional).

Blueberry Pancakes

CYNTHIA KELLER

These fluffy pancakes are delicious with just a pat of sweet butter and pure maple syrup. For extra sensorial gratification, try them with Jamie Roraback's Orange Flavored Maple Syrup on page 18.

MAKES ABOUT 12 PANCAKES

1 ½ cups sifted flour
2 ½ teaspoons baking powder
¼ teaspoon salt
1 egg, beaten

1 ½ cups milk
3 tablespoons melted unsalted butter
1 cup blueberries
Vegetable oil for greasing griddle

Combine the flour, baking powder and salt in a mixing bowl. Beat the eggs, milk and melted butter in another bowl until well combined.

Stir the egg mixture into the dry ingredients and gently fold until just combined. Do not over mix the batter or the pancakes will be tough and chewy. Fold in the blueberries.

Heat a nonstick griddle over medium-high heat. Lightly grease with the vegetable oil. Ladle about ½ cup batter onto the griddle for each pancake.

Cook until the bottom is golden brown and small bubbles appear on the surface. Flip over and continue cooking for about 30 seconds.

Remove to an oven-proof plate and keep warm in a 200° F oven until ready to serve.

Chef
Cynthia Keller

CHEF/OWNER
in Chester, Connecticut

Country French in Connecticut

You'll find her at *Restaurant du Village* in the quaint town of Chester, where she shares the stove with her husband, Michel. Upon graduation from cooking school, Cynthia honed her craft in some of the best kitchens on the East Coast, including the legendary Le Cirque in New York City.

The Draw of the Outdoors

Aside from their shared love of cooking, these two are passionate about the outdoors and all activities associated with it, from biking and canoeing to fishing and hiking.

Most Memorable Trip

Shortly after they met while living and cooking in New York City, working long hours at a very demanding pace, the couple took a two-week road trip through Alaska. They were enchanted by the beauty of Homer on the Kachemak Bay and its surroundings. And, as chefs, they especially remember the halibut cheeks and fresh-off-the-boat shrimp they often purchased and prepared simply for supper.

Least Romantic Trip

To celebrate their first-year anniversary, Cynthia and Michel took a short camping trip to renew their commitment to nature and to each other. Their dog, Cliquot, came along. Unfortunately, unbeknownst to the happy couple, they pitched their tent in the middle of a porcupine colony wanting to feast on the remains of their chicken curry. The terrorized dog spent the night growling, wedged between the two of them.

Dream Trip

Upon retiring, an event that selfish gourmets hope won't occur anytime soon, the intrepid pair is planning to buy an RV and explore Europe following all the national bicycle races, big and small, taking place throughout the continent. On the list so far: the Tour de France, Giro d'Italia and Vuelta a España.

In Her Backpack

She carries homemade granola and energy cookie bars made with oatmeal and nuts, and a small bag of all-around spice blend that usually includes Old Bay, curry and chili powder for quick seasoning.

Best Advice for the Outdoor Cook

Before you pack—unpack! Upon returning from shopping, she usually opens every package and box, measures what she needs and pours into small zipper bags. She also portions out any meat she plans to take along. It minimizes waste and takes up almost no space at all.

Restaurant du Village

59 Main Street
Chester, CT 06412
860-526-5301
WWW.RESTAURANTDUVILLAGE.COM

Banana Stuffed French Toast with Orange Maple Syrup

JAMIE RORABACK

For a nice change of pace from ho-hum breakfast fare, this tasty French toast is guaranteed to wake up your taste buds. The orange-flavored maple syrup is quite aromatic; you may consider making a double batch to use on other breakfast treats.

FOUR SERVINGS

1 orange
1 cup pure maple syrup
4 large eggs
1 cup heavy cream, half and half or milk
1 tablespoon pure vanilla extract

1 teaspoon ground cinnamon
Four 1-inch thick slices country white, wheat or raisin bread
1 banana, peeled and cut into ½-inch slices
2 tablespoons butter

Using a vegetable peeler, remove the orange rind. Place the rind in a small saucepan along with the maple syrup. Bring to a simmer and cook over low heat for 15 minutes. Strain the mixture in a bowl; discard the orange rind. Set aside to cool. This can be done ahead of time; refrigerate until ready to use.

In a shallow bowl, whisk together the eggs, cream, vanilla and cinnamon until smooth and well blended.

Cut the bread slices horizontally, leaving one edge still attached. Stuff with a few banana slices, making sure not to overstuff. Gently press down on the bread to enclose the banana slices. Soak the stuffed bread slices in the egg mixture for 2 minutes on each side.

Meanwhile, melt the butter in a griddle or nonstick pan over medium-low heat. Add the bread slices and cook gently for 4 to 5 minutes per side. Serve immediately with the orange maple syrup, seasonal fresh fruit, powdered sugar and whipped cream.

Seasonal Fresh Fruit with Lemon Curd Dip

JAMIE RORABACK

Here is a tangy recipe to liven up a platter of assorted fresh fruit. The curd is equally delicious spread on toast, or with cookies and a warm cup of tea as an afternoon snack.

FOUR SERVINGS

3 large eggs, beaten
1 egg yolk, beaten
1 cup sugar
8 tablespoons unsalted butter

3 oz freshly squeezed lemon juice
3 cups sliced fresh fruits: apples,
   peaches, pears or berries

Combine the eggs, egg yolk, sugar and butter in a heavy bottom, non-aluminum saucepan. Cook, whisking constantly, over medium heat until the mixture thickens to a thin pudding constancy, about 5 minutes. Do not let the mixture boil or it will curdle.

Pour the mixture into a shallow serving bowl. Cover the surface of the curd with plastic wrap to prevent a skin from forming. Refrigerate until completely chilled. Once chilled, the curd can be stored in a jar and kept refrigerated, covered, for up to 2 weeks.

Serve as a dipping sauce with sliced fresh fruits, cookies or toast.

Honey Vanilla Granola

CYNTHIA KELLER

Cynthia developed this granola as a nutritious snack to take along on her hiking adventures. It is also a very satisfying breakfast stirred in plain yogurt.

MAKES ABOUT 10 CUPS

5 cups old-fashioned oats
2 cups wheat bran
½ cup flax seeds
1 ½ cups whole almonds
1 ½ cups pecan halves

2 teaspoons cinnamon
1 ½ teaspoons vanilla extract
5 tablespoons canola oil
¾ cup honey
2 cups dried cranberries

Preheat the oven to 300° F.

Lightly grease 2 cookie sheets with oil spray.

Place the oats, wheat bran and flax seeds in a large bowl. Coarsely chop the almonds and pecans into chunky spoon-size pieces and add them to the grains. Sprinkle the cinnamon and stir to combine.

Combine the canola oil, honey and vanilla in a mixing bowl and stir until well blended. Pour the mixture over the grains and nuts and stir to coat evenly. The mixture will be somewhat sticky.

Divide the mixture among the 2 prepared cookie sheets. Spread out in an even layer. Bake for 1 hour, gently stirring every 15 minutes until the oats are toasted. Remove from oven and stir in dried cranberries. Allow to cool and store in an airtight container.

Planning Ahead

"When planning a trip, most people know what to pack for clothing and accessories. But when it comes to planning and packing food they are lost. It's so easy: you know how many days you'll be on the road and how many meals you'll need to provide—usually three a day: breakfast, lunch and dinner. Plan your menus one to two weeks before you go, then shop and pack accordingly."

"To minimize storage space and wasting food, plan on using certain staples twice during your trip. For example, if you pack a box of rice, serve a risotto one day and make a side dish a few days later with the leftover uncooked rice."

—Daniel Bruce

Super

SOUPS AND SANDWICHES

2

Sloppy Joes with Summer Corn on the Cob

ZAK PELACCIO

At most summertime picnics, cookouts and gatherings, Sloppy Joes are the ultimate treat, especially for children. Here is Zak's own twist on the classic sandwich.

SIX SERVINGS

5 bacon slices
1 ½ lbs ground beef
1 onion, minced
4 garlic cloves, minced
1 carrot, minced
3 tablespoons tomato paste
½ cup ketchup
2 tablespoons red wine vinegar

2 tablespoons soy sauce
1 tablespoon sugar
2 bay leaves
1 pinch chili flakes or more to taste
Salt and freshly ground pepper
   to taste
6 hamburger buns, lightly toasted
6 ears of corn, shucked

Heat a heavy skillet over high heat. Add the bacon slices and cook until some of the fat renders and the strips are crisp. Remove from the pan and set aside.

Add the ground beef and brown, stirring and breaking it up into pieces with a wooden spoon. Remove the meat from the pan and set aside.

Add the onion, garlic and carrot and lower the heat to medium. Sauté the vegetables, scraping the bottom of the pan, until lightly browned. Break the bacon into small pieces and return to the pan along with the ground meat. Add the tomato paste, ketchup, vinegar, soy sauce, sugar, bay leaves and chili flakes and simmer for 15 minutes. Adjust seasoning with salt and pepper to taste.

Meanwhile, bring a large pot of lightly salted water to a boil. Add the corn, cover and cook for approximately 6 to 7 minutes. Turn off the heat.

Pile the Sloppy Joe mixture onto the toasted roll bottoms and cover with the tops. Serve with the hot corn, butter and salt.

Grilled Country Bread with Native Tomatoes, Basil and Fresh Mozzarella

JAMIE RORABACK

A few years ago on a camping trip, Jamie proposed to his girlfriend over these luscious crostini. But, really, you don't need a special occasion to enjoy them. They are the essence of summer.

FOUR SERVINGS

4 slices country bread, about ¾-inch thick
½ cup olive oil
2 garlic cloves, peeled and halved lengthwise
4 thick slices fresh mozzarella

12 slices native tomatoes, about ½-inch thick
½ cup thinly shredded fresh basil
Salt and freshly ground black pepper to taste

Preheat the grill to medium. You can also use a broiler.

Place the bread slices on a cookie sheet and brush both sides with some olive oil. Reserve the remaining olive oil. Place the bread slices on the grill or under the broiler and toast for about 1½ minutes on each side or until deep golden on both sides. Remove from the heat, return to the cookie sheet and cool slightly.

Generously rub each slice with the garlic halves on one side and sprinkle with salt and black pepper. Top with a mozzarella slice and place the pan on the grill; cover the grill, and cook for 1½ minutes just to warm the cheese. Remove the pan from the grill and top each crostini with 3 slices of tomato and a sprinkling of fresh basil. Drizzle with the remaining olive oil, season with salt and pepper and serve immediately.

Connecticut Lobster and Basil Butter Crostini

JAMIE RORABACK

If you find yourself away from New England's rocky shores, steamed shrimp and even crab meat are good substitutes for these delectable open-face sandwiches. They are great on their own as an appetizer or with lightly dressed greens for a light meal for two.

FOUR SERVINGS

One 1 ½ lb lobster, cooked
1 French bread, cut into twelve
  ½-inch slices
8 tablespoons butter, melted
2 tablespoons thinly sliced basil
  leaves

Salt and freshly ground black pepper
  to taste
1 ½ cups thinly shredded green leaf
  lettuce

Crack the lobster shell and remove the tail and claw meat. Cut the meat into ¼-inch dice.

Heat the grill to medium-high. You can also use a broiler.

Place the slices of bread on a cookie sheet and brush with the melted butter on both sides. Reserve the remaining butter. Place the bread slices on the grill or under the broiler and cook for about 1 minute on each side until golden and lightly charred. Remove and place the bread on the cookie sheet.

Heat the remaining butter in a saucepan. Stir in the basil and lobster meat and season to taste with salt and pepper. Cook over medium heat, stirring once in a while, just to warm the lobster and coat it with the butter and basil. Do not overcook.

To assemble the crostini, place a small mound of lettuce on each bread slices and top with the hot lobster. Serve immediately.

Steak Po-Boy

JIMMY BANNOS

Serve Jimmy's scrumptious version of the New Orleans' classic sandwich with a side of Tangy Vegetable Slaw (page 140). For best results, marinate the meat overnight to permeate it with all the spicy flavors.

FOUR SERVINGS

Four ½-inch thick strip steaks (about 6 to 8 oz each), trimmed of excess fat
¼ cup Worcestershire sauce
2 to 3 tablespoons olive oil
1 garlic clove, crushed
2 large green or red bell peppers (or 1 of each), seeded and cut into 6 wedges

Four ¼-inch thick slices, cut from a large yellow onion
1 teaspoon Creole seasoning (see note)
¼ teaspoon ground black pepper
4 slices Swiss, Muenster or Provolone cheese
4 hoagie or medium size sandwich rolls, split lengthwise

Note: Creole seasoning is a spice blend available in most supermarkets. There are many varieties but it usually includes cayenne pepper, paprika and dried herbs such as garlic, thyme and oregano.

Place the steaks in a plastic zipper closure bag; add the Worcestershire sauce, 1 tablespoon olive oil and the crushed garlic. Seal and shake the bag to distribute the ingredients evenly. Marinate for at least 20 minutes or overnight in a refrigerator.

Preheat the grill to medium-high.

Brush the bell peppers and onion slices with the remaining oil. Grill until soft and lightly browned, about 6 to 10 minutes. Transfer to a plate and cover with aluminum foil.

Remove the steaks from the bag and wipe off the excess marinade. Season the meat with Creole seasoning and ground pepper. Grill for 3 to 4 minutes, turn over and continue cooking 2 to 3 minutes. Place a slice of cheese on each steak and allow it to melt. Place the hoagie cut side down on the grill until lightly toasted and warm.

Place 1 steak on each roll, break up the slices of onions into rings and divide among each sandwich; top with bell pepper slices. Serve immediately.

Vegetable Quesadillas

MINUTEMEALS CHEFS

Keep a few stacks of flour tortillas and a couple of bags of shredded cheese on hand as they can be turned into all sorts of quick and easy meals. Serve these quesadillas as a light meal or snack, or for breakfast with a side of scrambled eggs. For a non-vegetarian version, toss shredded ham, smoked turkey or leftover grilled meats into the mix.

FOUR SERVINGS

1 small green pepper, chopped
½ medium red onion, chopped
1 medium zucchini, chopped
1 cup canned or frozen corn
  kernels, drained
1 teaspoon chili powder

Salt and freshly ground pepper
  to taste
12 flour tortillas
8 oz pre-shredded Mexican cheese
  blend or Cheddar cheese
Homemade or store-bought salsa

Preheat the oven to 350° F.

Place the chopped peppers and onion in a skillet along with ¼ cup water. Bring to a boil over high heat and cook until the vegetables soften, about 2 minutes. Stir in the zucchini, corn and chili powder. Cook for 2 to 3 minutes or until the vegetables are cooked but still crisp and the water has evaporated. Remove the pan from the heat. Season with salt and pepper to taste.

Arrange 4 tortillas on a large baking sheet. Divide half of the vegetable mixture among the tortillas and spread evenly. Sprinkle with half the cheese. Top with another tortilla, the remaining vegetables and cheese. Cover with the remaining tortillas, pressing down on the layers. Bake for 5 minutes or until the cheese is melted and the filling hot. Cut the tortillas into wedges and serve with salsa on the side.

Adapted from Minutemeals.com

TIP The vegetable filling may be prepared up to 3 days before serving or frozen for up to 1 month. Add ¼ to ½ cup of water to the mixture while reheating.

Grilled Lobster and Goat Cheese Quesadillas

CHEF HARRY

These quesadillas offer an intriguing combination of flavors to be paired with the Toasted Jalapeño, Tomatillo and Watermelon Salsa (page 189). Serve them with a mixed green salad as a main course or cut into wedges as a hors d'oeuvres.

FOUR SERVINGS

1 tablespoon olive oil
1 teaspoon soy sauce
1 garlic clove, minced
Juice of 1 lemon
Two 8 oz lobster tails, fresh or frozen
    and thawed (see note)

4 medium flour tortillas
12 to 16 oz fresh goat cheese
Olive or vegetable oil for brushing
    the quesadillas
Toasted jalapeño tomatillo and
    watermelon salsa (page 189)

Note: Frozen lobster tails can be purchased online at www.ottomanelli.com.

Preheat the grill to medium-high.

Combine the olive oil, soy sauce, garlic and lemon juice in a small mixing bowl.

Crack the lobster shells and remove the meat. Toss into the olive oil marinade and stir to coat evenly. Marinate for 5 to 10 minutes.

Place the lobster tails on the grill and cook for 4 minutes on one side. Flip the tails and cook for another 4 to 5 minutes until the center is no longer pink. Remove from the grill and set aside to cool. Cut the lobster tails into thin slices.

Divide the lobster slices among the tortillas, arranging them on the lower half of each one. Crumble the goat cheese over the lobster and fold the tortillas over to form semi circles. Brush lightly with oil.

Place the quesadillas on the grill and cook for just 1 to 2 minutes on each side, until the cheese is melted and the tortillas are golden brown and crisp. Serve immediately with the toasted jalapeño tomatillo and watermelon salsa.

Fried Egg and Spam Sandwiches

MOLLY CHAPPELLET

Over the years, Spam has become a staple in Molly's traveling pantry. She keeps a couple of cans handy for quick easy dinners and she highly recommends using good quality wheat berry bread and chili sauce. The ones listed below are time-honored family favorites. A glass of Chappellet Chenin Blanc is all that is needed to round out this tasty little meal.

TWO SERVINGS

One 12 oz can Spam
2 tablespoons vegetable or olive oil,
   or butter
8 slices Orowheat "wheat berry"
   bread

4 large eggs
Mayonnaise to taste
Chile sauce to taste, preferably Seyco
   Old Fashioned
Lettuce leaves

Cut the Spam into thick slices.

Heat the oil or butter in a large skillet over medium-high heat. Add the slices and fry until golden on both sides. Remove the Spam slices from the pan and blot with paper towels.

In the same pan, add the eggs 1 at a time and fry, breaking the yolks with a fork as they cook. Do not overcook.

Lightly toast the bread slices. Spread 1 side of 4 toasts with a generous layer of mayonnaise. Spread the remaining toasts with the chile sauce. Layer the Spam slices, eggs and some lettuce leaves on top of the 4 mayonnaise toasts. Cover with the remaining chile coated ones and serve immediately.

Molly Chappellet

CO-OWNER CHAPPELLET WINERY
IN NAPA VALLEY, AND AUTHOR

Napa Style

Molly's reputation as a superlative cook and celebrated hostess expands far beyond her winery perched in Pritchard's Hill. Over the years, her lavish table settings and centerpieces and straightforward but flavorful dishes inspired by her award-winning gardens have left guests raving.

RVing for Love

Because her husband Donn loves to drive and seems happiest behind the wheel, Molly suggested getting a little house attached to their car. Ten years and three coaches later, the couple tries to steal three to four road trips a year from their demanding schedule.

Freedom of the Road

A perfectionist and formidable organizer, Molly leaves it all behind once they hit the highway. They seldom plan ahead, preferring to let their imagination and curiosity lead them to the most remote places.

Favorite Places to Pull Up

They often travel south to Palm Springs, stopping to visit friends along the way. And exploring the wonders of the High Sierras is one of the couple frequent adventures.

Simplicity on the Road

The free-spirited, relaxed approach to travel and leisure is evident in their roving kitchen. "When we started, we were more ambitious and quite elaborate with our meals," says Molly. Today, they simply throw a few ingredients together in a crockpot before going off on their adventures or assemble a colorful, delectable salad of garden fresh vegetables upon their return.

In Their Pantry

As winemakers and arbiters of taste, Molly and Donn, also a superb cook, know that quality ingredients are the answer to pleasurable, easy dining. They carry artisanal local cheeses, a selection of nuts and dried fruits for snacks or impromptu salads; fruits and vegetables from their garden; assorted condiments such as local olive oils, capers and mustards; smoked salmon; and for emergencies, Wolfgang Puck's canned soups, Spam, and frozen meals. And a well-stocked wine cellar, of course.

Book Stash:

A Vineyard Garden: Ideas From the Earth for Growing, Cooking and Entertaining. Molly Chappellet. Introduction by Hugh Johnson (Viking Studio Books, 1991).

The Romance of California Vineyards. Molly Chappellet & Carissa Chappellet. Photography by Daniel D'Agostini (Universe Publishing, 1997).

Gardens of the Wine Country. Molly Chappellet with Richard Tracy (Chronicle Books, 1998).

Chappellet Winery

1581 Sage Canyon Road
St. Helena, CA 94574
707-963-7136 or 1-800-4-WINERY
WWW.CHAPPELLET.COM

"Barbecue" Pulled Pork

JACK HIGGINS

Jack Higgins is the creative culinary mind behind Starwich, an innovative upscale dining concern sprouting up around the country. Starwich's impressive selection of sophisticated sandwiches features market-fresh produce and top of the line ingredients. Jack agreed to share his terrific "barbecue" pulled pork sandwich, which does not require smoke, tears or sweat. Serve with crispy onion rings and his Tangy Vegetable Slaw on page 140.

SIX TO EIGHT SERVINGS

3 lbs pork butt
1 drop liquid smoke (optional)
Kaiser rolls

BARBECUE SAUCE:
32 oz ketchup
¾ cup honey
¼ cup cider vinegar
1 teaspoon brown sugar
¼ teaspoon smoky paprika
¼ teaspoon chili powder
1 small onion, finely minced
4 garlic cloves, finely minced
⅛ teaspoon dry mustard
½ teaspoon Worcestershire sauce

Combine all the ingredients for the barbeque sauce in a mixing bowl. Stir well to blend.

Rinse the pork butt under cold running water. Pat dry and place in a crock pot. Add 2 cups barbeque sauce and coat the meat evenly. Add 2 cups water and the liquid smoke (optional); cover and cook for 8 hours on low setting.

Remove the meat from the pot and cool slightly. Shred the meat with a fork, discarding any fat and gristle. Stir in some barbeque sauce to taste.

Toast the Kaiser rolls and top with the shredded meat and tangy vegetable slaw. Serve with crispy onion rings, if desired, and extra sauce on the side.

Goat Cheese Monte Cristo Sandwiches

NEAL FRASER

This recipe is a lovely variation on the Monte Cristo sandwich and is somewhat lighter than its classic counterpart. The tart goat cheese and fresh herbs give this sandwich a pleasing lively tang. Use any herb combination available. Neal recommends serving them with a bowl of Roasted Tomato and Piquillo Pepper Soup on page 39.

SIX SERVINGS

12 slices brioche or good quality firm white bread, about ½-inch thick
6 oz fresh goat cheese, softened
¼ cup loosely packed chopped mixed herbs: parsley, basil, chives, tarragon, etc.
Salt and freshly ground pepper to taste

2 large eggs
¼ cup milk
1 cup flour
1 small bag of panko (Japanese bread crumbs) or regular bread crumbs
¼ cup canola or vegetable oil

Remove the crust from the brioche or bread and lay the slices on a work surface.

Blend the goat cheese with the herbs in a mixing bowl and season to taste with salt and pepper. Generously spread 1 side of 6 slices with the mixture. Top with the remaining slices, pressing gently to secure. Set aside until ready to cook.

Beat the eggs and milk in a shallow bowl and season with salt and pepper. Spread the flour on a plate and the bread crumbs on another.

Heat the oil in a nonstick frying pan over medium-high heat. Lightly coat the sandwiches with the flour, shaking off the excess. Then, dip both sides into the egg mixture. Coat the sandwiches on both sides with the bread crumbs.

When the oil is hot but not smoking, add 3 sandwiches (depending on the size of the pan) to the pan and cook for 2 minutes; gently flip on the other side and cook until golden brown, about 4 minutes. Drain on paper towel. Repeat with the remaining sandwiches. Cut the sandwiches in half on the bias and serve with the roasted tomato soup.

Truffle Grilled Cheese Sandwiches

NEAL FRASER

For many epicureans, toasted country bread spread with sweet butter and showered with thinly sliced fresh truffles is the ultimate sandwich. Neal's version is much more democratic and easier on the wallet. He tells us that melted truffle cheese on rye is simply the best—we think you'll agree.

SIX SERVINGS

12 slices good quality rye bread
6 tablespoons unsalted butter, room
   temperature
6 oz truffle cheese, thinly sliced
   (see note)

Note: Truffle cheese is imported from Italy and is available in specialty cheese shops. It can also be purchased online. See the resource page 202.

Spread both sides of the rye bread slices with butter.

Layer the cheese on top of 6 slices and top with the remaining slices.

Heat a heavy skillet over medium-high heat. Add the truffle sandwiches and cook until golden on one side. Flip the sandwiches and cook until the cheese is melted and the bread nicely toasted. Serve immediately.

Packing a Cooler

Jamie Roraback recommends using two coolers well stocked with ice, preferably blue ice. Use one cooler for beverages and ready to eat foods that do not require cooking. Always use a separate cooler to hold any raw meats to prevent cross-contamination. You never want meat juices dripping onto foods that will not be cooked such as produce, tops of beverage containers, etc. Keep a refrigerator thermometer inside to ensure a constant temperature of 40° F or below and refrain from opening the cooler too often.

Asparagus Soup with Porcini Mushroom Essence

NEAL FRASER

Asparagus and mushrooms have a natural affinity. Here Neal uses dried porcini as a flavoring for the delicate soup. You can substitute your favorite dried mushrooms such as morels, chanterelles or shitake.

SIX TO EIGHT SERVINGS

⅛ oz dried porcini mushrooms
¾ cup nonfat milk
3 tablespoons olive oil
1 medium white onion,
  thinly sliced

4 celery stalks, chopped
4 cups chicken or vegetable broth
1 large bunch asparagus, about
  1 ½ lbs, peeled and chopped
Kosher salt to taste

Place the porcini mushrooms in a small saucepan. Add the milk and bring to a simmer. Remove from the heat and let it steep for 20 minutes. Puree the mixture in a blender and strain through a fine mesh strainer. Season with salt and pepper and refrigerate until ready to use. This can be done up to 1 day ahead.

Heat the oil in a stock pot over medium-low heat. Add the onions and cook until soft and translucent, about 5 minutes. Do not brown. Add the celery and some salt. Continue cooking until the vegetables are soft, about 5 minutes. Add the broth and bring to a boil. Cover, lower the heat and simmer for 20 minutes.

Add the chopped asparagus to the pot, cover and simmer for 20 minutes until the vegetables are very soft. Puree the mixture in a blender and return to the pot. Adjust seasoning to taste with salt. This can be done ahead and refrigerated until ready to serve.

To serve, reheat the soup and ladle into serving bowls. Swirl some porcini cream into each serving.

Roasted Tomato and Piquillo Peppers Soup

NEAL FRASER

Piquillo peppers are slightly spicy peppers from Spain. They are excellent tossed into salads, seafood and chicken stews. In Spain, they are often served as part of a tapas spread with chunks of cheese, olives, sausages and other delicacies to be savored with small glasses of wine.

SIX TO EIGHT SERVINGS

20 plum tomatoes, halved
4 tablespoons butter
1 yellow onion, coarsely chopped
4 garlic cloves, minced
1 carrot, chopped

One 8 oz jar roasted piquillo peppers (see note)
6 cups chicken broth
Salt and freshly ground pepper to taste

Note: Piquillo peppers are available in specialty gourmet stores and upscale supermarkets or can be purchased online. See resource page 202.

Preheat the oven to 450° F.

Place the tomatoes on a roasting pan and roast for 10 to 15 minutes until dark golden and slightly charred. This can also be done on the grill. Set aside.

Combine the butter and onion in a deep, heavy pot and place over medium-low heat. Cook, stirring once in a while, until the onions are soft and caramelized, about 5 minutes. Add the garlic and carrot to the pot and cook for another 3 minutes. Add the chicken stock, roasted tomatoes, piquillo peppers and salt to taste. Bring to a boil, reduce the heat and simmer for 1 hour.

Puree the soup in a blender and strain through a fine meshed strainer. Adjust seasoning with salt and pepper to taste. Reheat the soup just before serving.

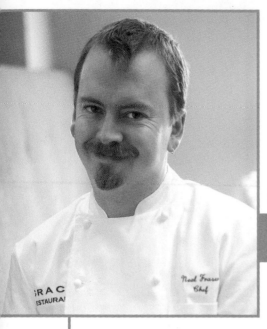

Chef
Neal Fraser

EXECUTIVE CHEF/PARTNER,
Grace Restaurant, Los Angeles, California

Trailing Neal

With the opening of Grace Restaurant, Neal realized a long-time dream of showcasing his contemporary American fare that is nuanced and accessible, yet full of ambitious flavors in a casually elegant setting. Early on in his career, Neal's modern American cuisine and his prolific creativity put him on the critics' watch list. Soon the visionary chef was considered "one of Los Angeles' most revolutionary culinary talents." Outside of his kitchen, you can catch him on the Food Network as an occasional challenger on *Iron Chef America*.

Outdoor Life

Intense and focused in the kitchen, once he hangs up his chef's jacket this native Los Angelino embraces the laid back California lifestyle with abandon—especially when it comes to outdoor activities. An enthusiastic and dedicated cyclist, Neal has taken many extended camping trips on two wheels up and down the coast of Southern California. Today with the demanding schedule of being a father and running a restaurant, his outings are few and far between but his spirit remains.

A Man on Fire

A couple of years ago, he and his wife, Amy, joined a group of friends on their way to the Burning Man Project, a festival held annually in the Black Rock Desert. Started in San Francisco as a small community event, the week-long event attracts as many as 25,000 people from every part of the country and the world. Neal was quite taken by the whole experience — the fun free-spirited camaraderie, the art exhibits, music and dance performances, and street theater. By default, Neil was responsible for the meals as none of his reveler friends cooked. So he fed ten people a day from his well-stocked coolers. And if the recipes he contributed to this book are any indication, they must have eaten pretty well!

The Ultimate Fantasy

After experiencing the Burning Man Project and its many levels of creativity, Neal is planning to attend the yearly event again. And he hopes to enter someday as a participating artist and create an installation of his own. For a week, in his 15-seat ephemeral restaurant, this culinary performer will let his imagination run wild with his cuisine, engaging and seducing his captive audience. For now, it is a fantasy. But stay tuned!

Grace Restaurant

7360 Beverly Boulevard
Los Angeles, CA 90036
323-934-4400
WWW.GRACERESTAURANT.COM

English Pea and Soy Bean Soup

NEAL FRASER

Can't get easier than this healthy vibrant soup! Thick and creamy without the cream, it makes for a satisfying lunch or pleasing first course. For an elegant presentation, garnish with snippets of fresh chives or mint, a dollop of sour cream or crumbled bacon left over from breakfast.

SIX TO EIGHT SERVINGS

3 tablespoons olive oil
1 large white onion, thinly sliced
2 cups chopped celery
6 cups chicken or vegetable broth

3 cups frozen English peas
3 cups frozen soy beans (edamame)
Kosher salt to taste

Heat the olive oil over medium-low heat in a deep saucepan. Add the onion and cook until soft and translucent, about 5 minutes. Do not brown. Add the celery and salt; cook for another 4 minutes.

When the vegetables are soft, add the stock and bring to a boil. Lower the heat and simmer for 20 minutes.

Add the peas and soy beans and bring back to a boil. Lower the heat and simmer for 10 to 15 minutes, until tender.

Puree the mixture in a blender. Strain the soup using a fine mesh strainer (optional). Return to the pot and adjust seasoning with salt to taste. Add a little water or broth if the consistency is too thick to your taste. Just before serving, reheat the soup and serve immediately.

Roasted Butternut Squash and Coconut Soup

NEAL FRASER

This soup is both delicate and fragrant; each flavor is apparent without overpowering the others. Neal likes to serve this soup topped with sautéed sweet shrimp from Maine. Do not worry if you can't find any (the season is very brief); this soup doesn't need any embellishment.

SIX SERVINGS

1 ½ lb butternut squash, split in half lengthwise and seeded
3 tablespoons canola or vegetable oil
1 large white onion, chopped
1 carrot, chopped

One 14 oz can unsweetened coconut milk
5 to 6 cups chicken stock
One 1-inch piece ginger, peeled
1 stalk lemon grass, halved
Salt to taste

Preheat the oven to 350° F.

Rub the squash with 1 tablespoon of oil and place cut side down on a baking sheet. Roast until the flesh is soft, about 1 hour. Remove from the oven and cool. When cool enough to handle, scoop out the flesh.

In a large saucepan, heat 2 tablespoons oil over low heat. Add the onion, cover and sweat until translucent, 3 to 5 minutes. Add the carrots and cook for another 5 minutes.

Add the coconut milk, 5 cups of chicken stock, the ginger, lemon grass and roasted squash. Season with salt and bring to a simmer. Cook for 1 hour.

Discard the ginger and lemongrass and puree in a blender or food processor. Add some chicken stock if the soup is too thick. Adjust seasoning to taste with salt and pepper. Reheat if necessary and serve immediately.

TIP The soup can be partially prepared ahead and frozen until ready to serve. Follow the instructions to the end of the recipe but omit the coconut milk. When ready to serve, defrost and add the coconut milk to the soup base and simmer for 10 minutes. Add some chicken broth if the soup is too thick. Adjust seasoning with salt and pepper and serve.

Roasted Potato, Bacon and Cheddar Soup

JAMIE RORABACK

Although roasting the potatoes and onions for this soup may seem a little superfluous, it is well worth the effort. The result is a creamy mellow soup with a hint of sweetness to complement the smokiness of the bacon.

FOUR SERVINGS

8 bacon slices
4 medium potatoes, unpeeled and cut
   into ½-inch dice
1 large onion, cut into ½-inch dice
4½ cups chicken or vegetable broth
½ cup grated cheddar cheese

4 tablespoons chopped scallions
   or chives
½ cup heavy cream or milk (optional)
Salt and freshly ground black
   pepper to taste
Chopped scallions, shredded cheddar
   and croutons for garnish

Preheat the oven to 450° F.

Cook the bacon in a skillet until crisp. Remove from the pan and reserve the fat. Cut the bacon into ¼-inch pieces and reserve.

Coat the diced potatoes and onion with 2 to 3 tablespoons of the reserved bacon fat and spread in a single layer on a cookie sheet.

Roast in oven, stirring occasionally, for 20 to 30 minutes or until golden brown.

Transfer the roasted potatoes and onions to a large saucepan. Add the broth, season with salt, cover and bring to a simmer. Cook over medium heat for 20 minutes.

Using a potato masher, puree the mixture until nearly smooth. For a creamier texture, use an immersion mixer or blender. Return the soup to the pot and bring back to a simmer over medium heat. Gradually whisk in the cheddar cheese. If soup is too thick, stir in more broth or water to the desired consistency.

Stir in the scallions, reserved bacon pieces and the heavy cream or milk (optional). Adjust seasoning with salt and black pepper to taste. Serve immediately with assorted garnishes.

Steamed Littleneck and Native Sweet Corn Chowder

JAMIE RORABACK

Sweet corn and briny clams have a natural affinity and for many gourmands they epitomize the flavors of summer. Jamie's version of the New England chowder is lighter than traditional recipes and boasts sweeter, more delicate flavors. This recipe yields 4 servings as an elegant first course, double the recipe for a more substantial main course.

FOUR SERVINGS

2 tablespoons butter
1 medium onion, diced (about 1 cup)
4 to 5 small red potatoes, diced (about 1 ½ cups)
2 teaspoons fresh thyme leaves
¼ cup white wine, preferably a sweeter variety such as Riesling
¾ cup water
24 littleneck clams, washed to remove any sand
1 cup fresh corn kernels
½ cup milk or half and half
Salt and freshly ground pepper to taste

Melt the butter over medium-low heat in a large saucepan. Add the onions, potatoes and thyme and cook, covered, for about 5 minutes or until the onions are soft and translucent and the potatoes start to become tender. Do not brown.

Increase the heat to high, add the white wine and boil for 30 seconds. Add the water, clams and corn kernels. Cover and simmer for about 5 minutes or until the clams are opened and potatoes cooked through.

Scoop out the clams and divide among 4 serving bowls. Pour the milk or half and half into the pot and bring to a simmer. Season to taste with pepper and, if necessary, some salt. Simmer for 2 minutes.

Ladle the broth, potatoes and corn over the clams and serve with oyster crackers.

3
Easy Does It
DISHES FOR SKILLETS AND STEW POTS

Chicken in Hunter-Style Sauce

TOM VALENTI

Although this stew is very easy to assemble and contains very few ingredients, it has a great depth of flavors. Tom suggests serving it with orzo, the rice-shaped Greek pasta. Quick cooking couscous or buttery mashed potatoes are also good options.

FOUR SERVINGS

2 to 3 very ripe large tomatoes or 1 cup canned Italian plum tomatoes
Coarse salt to taste
Freshly ground black pepper to taste
4 whole chicken legs
¼ cup olive oil

1 medium Spanish onion, peeled and cut into 8 wedges
3 garlic cloves, thinly sliced
1 cup dry white wine
1 cup dry Vermouth
¼ cup fresh oregano leaves

If using fresh tomatoes, about 30 minutes before cooking, cut the tomatoes into large pieces and put in a bowl. Season with salt and pepper, give a good toss and set aside at room temperature.

Preheat the oven to 375° F.

Season the chicken pieces generously with salt and pepper. Heat the olive oil in a large heavy pot over medium-high heat until hot but not smoking. Add the chicken pieces and brown for 4 to 5 minutes on each side. Remove from the pan and set aside. Add the onion and garlic to the pot and stir, until softened, about 6 minutes. Add the reserved tomatoes (or canned tomatoes) and their juices and cook for 1 minute. Add the wine, vermouth and oregano, and bring to a boil.

Return the chicken pieces to the pot, skin side up. Cover and cook in the oven for 40 minutes or until cooked through. Divide the chicken pieces among 4 serving plates and spoon the sauce over them. Serve immediately.

Recipe adapted from Soups, Stews and One-Pot Meals. Tom Valenti and Andrew Friedman (Scribner, 2003)

TIP   If you find yourself with leftovers, cut the chicken into bite size pieces and simmer in the sauce just to warm up. Toss over fettuccini and top with freshly grated Parmesan cheese.

Chef
Tom Valenti

CHEF/OWNER
Ouest Restaurant, New York City

Tom's New York Trail

This chef has a definite knack for big satisfying flavors in his accessible yet sophisticated one-pot dishes. His stylish restaurant on Manhattan's Upper West Side serves serious French-inspired American fare in a casual "comfort zone" atmosphere. Early on, Tom worked under some of the city's best chefs, but quickly distinguished himself by his multi-layered homey style that left jaded New Yorkers swooning—not a small feat!

Open Roads

"It's a generation thing," says Tom. "There is a time in your life when, after proving yourself and working hard, you just look for some freedom." For him and his wife, Abigail, this freedom comes in the shape of an RV. Their dream is to take off someday for a long stretch of time and explore this country's backwoods. With the giddy excitement of teenagers, they have spent many hours debating possible destinations, interior decorating and, of course, recipes.

In Training

Their favorite recurring summer road trip takes them from San Francisco to Los Angeles along the rugged California central coast, with a few days of stopover at the rustic Deetjen Inn in Big Sur.

Before hopping into their vintage convertible, they pack a couple of coolers from their preferred food shops in San Francisco. Granted, this is not quite the RV experience but, hey, one has to start somewhere!

Further Training

An avid fly fisherman and all-around outdoor man, a few years ago Tom bought a three-room log cabin in the woods of the Catskills. His diminutive kitchen includes a non-working stove and no counter space; most meals are prepared outdoors on the grill.

What He'll Stow

So, in Tom's dream galley, you will definitely find a grill and a crockpot for his lusty soups and stews. He'll stock his pantry with cumin, cayenne pepper, fennel, mustard and coriander seeds, sherry wine vinegar and good olive oil. He loves to splash spicy mustard oil (available in most Indian stores) on practically everything from fish (fresh and smoked) to vegetables, steaks and chops. Last, the secret ingredient for his one-pot meals: plain white distilled vinegar! It lends brightness of flavor and depth and, unlike citrus juice or red wine vinegar, gives some acidity to braised dishes without conflicting flavors.

Book Stash

Tom Valenti's Soups, Stews and One-Pot Meals
by Tom Valenti and Andrew Friedman (Scribner, 2003)

Welcome to My Kitchen: A New York Chef Shares His Robust Recipes and Secret Techniques by Tom Valenti and Andrew Friedman (Morrow Cookbooks, 2002)

Ouest Restaurant

2315 Broadway
New York, NY 10024
212-580-8700
WWW.OUESTNY.COM

Chicken Curry

ZAK PELACCIO

Fragrant and easy to share, curries are the epitome of conviviality. To give this aromatic stew more opulence, Zak suggests adding diced seasonal vegetables such as eggplant, tomato, zucchini, red and green peppers, yellow squash or green beans to the sauce. You could also use shrimp instead of chicken. A word of caution: Thai and Serrano chiles are very hot, so carefully adjust the amount to your taste. If neither is available, substitute with ground cayenne pepper or crushed pepper flakes.

FOUR SERVINGS

1 small bunch cilantro
2 tablespoons vegetable oil
3 boneless, skinless chicken breasts, sliced crosswise into 1-inch pieces
1 onion, finely chopped
3 garlic cloves, minced
One 2-inch piece of ginger, peeled, halved lengthwise and lightly crushed
2 to 3 Thai or Serrano chiles, seeded and minced, or to taste
Juice of 2 limes
1 tablespoon sugar
2 tablespoons Vietnamese fish sauce (nuoc mam) or lite soy sauce

One 13.5 oz can unsweetened coconut milk
1 ½ to 2 cups chicken broth
3 cups steamed Jasmine rice

CURRY SPICE BLEND:
1 tablespoon ground coriander seeds
½ teaspoon ground cumin
½ teaspoon ground fennel seeds
½ teaspoon turmeric

Separate the cilantro leaves from the stems and set aside. Finely mince the stems.

Heat a large sauté pan over high heat. Add the oil and sear the chicken pieces until golden brown. Remove the chicken from the pan and set aside. Add the garlic, onion, ginger, minced cilantro stems and chili peppers to the pan. Cook, stirring once in a while, for 3 to 5 minutes or until the vegetables soften. Add the curry spice blend and cook, stirring for 2 minutes.

Return the chicken to the pan, add the juice of 1 lime, sugar, fish sauce or soy sauce, coconut milk and chicken broth. Bring to a boil, lower the heat to medium and simmer for 10 to 15 minutes. Adjust seasoning with the remaining lime juice and some fish sauce or salt to taste.

Divide the rice among 4 serving plates and spoon the chicken and curry sauce over. Garnish with the reserved cilantro leaves and lime wedges.

> TIP   Measure out and pack the spice blend in a small plastic bag or container before leaving on your trip. The blend can also be used as a rub on poultry, or as a seasoning for sautéed vegetables. Don't forget to label it.

Low-Carb Chicken Parmesan

FRANK OTTOMANELLI

This is a great recipe for anyone watching his or her waistline (or not) but not wanting to sacrifice taste.

SIX SERVINGS

6 boneless, skinless chicken breasts
Chef's salt to taste (see tip on
   page 99)
2 tablespoons olive oil
2 cups tomato sauce, homemade or
   store-bought

4 tablespoons chopped parsley
1 ½ teaspoons dried oregano
1 teaspoon garlic powder
1 teaspoon dried basil
½ cup grated Parmesan cheese
1 ½ cups shredded mozzarella cheese

Preheat the oven to 375° F.

Place one chicken breast between two pieces of plastic wrap. Using the flat side of a meat mallet or a small heavy saucepan, gently pound the breast to 1 ½-inch thickness. Repeat with the remaining breasts.

Arrange the breasts in a large baking dish in a single layer; sprinkle both sides with the chef's salt and drizzle with the olive oil to coat evenly.

Combine the tomato sauce with 3 tablespoons parsley, oregano, garlic powder, basil and Parmesan cheese in a mixing bowl. Season with some chef's salt. Spoon the sauce over the chicken breasts, ensuring they are evenly coated. Top each one with ¼ cup shredded mozzarella. Sprinkle with the remaining parsley.

Bake for 25 to 35 minutes until mozzarella is melted and golden brown. Remove from the oven and let rest for 5 to 10 minutes before serving.

Curried Rice with Chicken and Cauliflower

MELISSA PERELLO

Here is a one pot dish that delivers big flavors with minimum effort. Leftover grilled or roasted chicken can be used.

TWO SERVINGS

1 tablespoon butter or vegetable oil
1 small onion, finely minced
1 garlic clove, minced
1 teaspoon minced ginger
1 medium tomato, diced into ½-inch pieces
¾ cup coarsely chopped cauliflower
1 teaspoon Madras curry blend
¼ teaspoon ground cinnamon

Pinch cayenne pepper or to taste
2 boneless chicken breasts or thighs, 8 to 10 oz each
¾ cup long grain rice
1 chicken bouillon cube
1 tablespoon sliced and toasted almonds
1 tablespoon chopped golden raisins

Heat the butter or oil in a medium saucepan set over low heat. Add the onion, garlic and ginger and cook until translucent and soft, about 4 minutes. Do not brown.

Add the cauliflower, tomato and spices; cover and cook the vegetables slowly until tender and the tomato has broken down and becomes loose, about 15 minutes. This should be done over low heat. Remove the lid and allow any liquid to reduce for 3 to 4 more minutes. Season with salt to taste and remove the vegetables from the pan to cool.

Meanwhile, roast or sauté the chicken until cooked thoroughly. Cool and shred the meat and add it to the cooled vegetable mixture. This recipe can be prepared up to this point and refrigerated or frozen until ready to serve.

When ready to serve, combine the rice and bouillon cube with ¾ cup water in a small 1 to 2 quart pot; bring to a simmer, cover and cook for 8 to 10 minutes. Stir; add the vegetable and chicken mixture and continue cooking covered over a low flame for another 8 to 10 minutes or until rice is thoroughly cooked. Season to taste with salt and pepper and stir in the almonds and raisins to finish. Serve immediately.

TIP The recipe can be prepared through step 3, stored in a plastic freezer bag or container and refrigerated for up to 2 days or frozen for up to 1 month.

Poached Chicken Breasts with Spring Vegetables and Herb Broth

JAMIE RORABACK

Quick and easy, this aromatic recipe is perfect for a light supper. It is delicious served over couscous for a more substantial meal.

FOUR SERVINGS

4 cups low-sodium chicken broth
4 boneless and skinless chicken
  breasts, about 6 oz each
8 to 10 pearl onions, peeled
2 carrots, cut into ¾-inch pieces
8 asparagus spears, cut crosswise
  into 1-inch pieces

2 tablespoons cold butter
3 tablespoons minced mixed fresh
  herbs: Italian parsley, tarragon,
  chives, etc.
Salt and black pepper to taste

Bring the chicken broth to a simmer in a shallow saucepan large enough to hold the chicken breasts in a single layer.

Rinse the chicken breasts and pat dry. Season on both sides with salt and pepper. Add the breasts and pearl onions to the broth and bring back to a simmer; lower the heat and gently poach for 10 minutes. Add the carrots and asparagus and cook for 8 to 10 minutes, or until the chicken is cooked through and the vegetables tender.

Remove the chicken breasts and vegetables from the broth with a slotted spoon and divide among 4 shallow bowls.

Whisk the butter into the broth and adjust seasoning with salt and pepper to taste. Ladle over the chicken breasts; sprinkle each serving with the mixed herbs and serve with the remaining broth on the side.

How to Safely Handle Fresh or Frozen Meats

Always keep the meat refrigerated or frozen before using and slowly thaw the meat in the refrigerator. It may take 3 to 4 days depending on the density of the cut, so plan accordingly. If time is an issue, place in the microwave and thaw using the defrost function.

Always keep raw meat and poultry separated from other foods. Wash working surfaces including cutting boards, utensils and hands after touching raw meat or poultry. You may consider investing in two cutting boards and dedicate one of them for meat only.

Always cook meat thoroughly or to desired doneness. Immediately refrigerate leftovers or discard.

—Frank Ottomanelli

Chicken Cordon Bleu

CRAIG SHELTON

French fries or herb-roasted potatoes are the obvious sidekicks for this Franco-American classic, but for a more unusual pairing, try Daniel Bruce's Barbecue Corn on the Cob on page 152, or Neal Fraser's Corn and Potato "Risotto" on page 151.

FOUR SERVINGS

4 boneless, skinless chicken breasts
Salt and freshly ground pepper
   to taste
4 slices smoked ham
4 slices Provolone cheese or melting
   cheese such as Swiss
1 cup bread crumbs

¼ cup Parmesan cheese
½ cup flour
2 large eggs, beaten
5 tablespoons butter
1 cup chicken stock
Lemon juice to taste

Preheat the oven to 350° F.

Place one chicken breast between 2 pieces of plastic wrap. Using the flat side of a meat mallet or a small heavy saucepan, gently pound the breast to ¼-inch thickness, making sure not to tear the meat. Repeat with the remaining breasts.

Season the breasts with salt and pepper on both sides. Layer a slice of ham over 1 side of each breast, followed by a slice of cheese. Tuck in the sides of the breasts to enclose the filling and roll like a jelly roll. Secure with a toothpick.

Combine the bread crumbs and Parmesan cheese and spread on a plate. Place the eggs in a shallow bowl, and season with salt and pepper. Spread the flour on a plate.

Heat 4 tablespoons butter in a large ovenproof skillet over medium-high heat.

Lightly dredge the chicken breasts in the flour to coat, shaking off the excess. Dip the breasts on all sides into the beaten eggs, then into the bread crumb mixture to coat evenly.

Add the chicken breasts to the skillet and sear until golden brown on all sides. Transfer the pan to the oven and bake for 15 to 20 minutes, until cooked through but not dry.

Meanwhile, reduce the chicken stock by ¼ in a small saucepan. Whisk in the remaining butter; season to taste with salt, pepper and lemon juice. Cut the chicken breasts into thick slices and arrange on a serving platter. Spoon some of the sauce over the slices and serve immediately.

Chef
Craig Shelton

CHEF/OWNER
The Ryland Inn, White House, New Jersey

Kitchen Experiment

Most of the time, you will find Craig in his sprawling laboratory kitchen, playing with flavors, ingredients and combinations to create his very personal and seasonal cuisine. Or you may find him in his four-acre organic garden, plucking herbs and selecting flawless vegetables for the evening's tasting menus.

What Do a Scientist and Chef Have in Common?

A lot more than you think—that is, if you're Craig Shelton, who received dual degrees in molecular biophysics and biochemistry from Yale University. Unfortunately, laboratories are not conducive to conviviality! From his grandmother, the owner of a small country restaurant in Cognac, France, he learned that cooking and great food bring joy into people's lives; an appealing concept he eventually decided to pursue. However, as a chef today, Craig approaches every dish with the same analytic, curious mind of the scientist he almost became.

First Cooking Accolade

Craig says that his father knew his son would eventually become a chef when the teenager planned Chicken Cordon Bleu, Cobb Salad and a cherry pie as part of his Boy Scout merit badge cooking test. "It wasn't difficult," brags the chef today. "The hard part was carrying everything in a backpack." He solved the problem by cleverly waiting to complete his assignment on the shortest hike of the season.

An RV with a Mast and Sail?

Although he has been known to enjoy occasional camping trips, in the past couple of years Craig has become an enthusiastic sailor, pulling up anchor as often as he can.

So What is He Doing in This Book?

According to this chef, cooking on a boat galley or in an RV kitchen requires the same skills and keen sense of organization and planning. He swears that RVers could learn a lot from sailors. Or could it be the other way around?

In His Galley

He stows coq au vin, cassoulet and steak sauce Bordelaise, along with a few bottles of vintage Bordeaux. Sound over the top? Well, you too could do the same if you had a staff of 20 cooks and sous-chefs prepping, cooking and packing for you!

The Ryland Inn

Route 22 West
White House, New Jersey 08888
908-534-4011
WWW.RYLANDINN.COM

Donn's Motorcoach Stew

MOLLY CHAPPELLET

When Donn and Molly are traveling in their motorhome, Donn likes to toss all the following ingredients into his crock pot, go off for the day and come back to a beautiful one-course meal. With this full flavored stew, the winemakers recommend their intensely aromatic Merlot or their impeccably balanced Chappellet Signature Cabernet Sauvignon.

FOUR SERVINGS

1 lb beef stew meat, trimmed and cut into 1-inch cubes

1 ½ lbs lamb stew meat, trimmed and cut into 1-inch cubes

Flour for dredging

½ lb sausage of choice, cut into bite size pieces

3 cups unpeeled, cubed new potatoes

1 large onion, cut into large chunks

2 cups diced carrots

One 28 oz can diced tomatoes

One 14 oz can beef broth

1 cup Chappellet red wine

¼ cup Herbes de Provence

½ teaspoon ground cinnamon

Dash of Tabasco sauce

1 teaspoon Lawry's or other seasoned salt

1 to 3 garlic cloves, crushed (optional)

2 bay leaves

2 cups mushrooms, trimmed and quartered

Freshly ground pepper to taste

Dust the beef and lamb pieces with a little flour.

Place the meat pieces along with the sausage, potatoes, onion, carrots, tomatoes, beef broth, red wine, Herbes de Provence, cinnamon, Tabasco, seasoned salt, garlic and bay leaves in crock pot or other slow cooker. Set the timer to low and cook for about 7 hours.

Add the mushrooms to the pot and stir to combine. Cover the pot and cook for another 2 hours.

Million Dollar Meatloaf

FRANK OTTOMANELLI

This moist and tasty meatloaf is delicious the next day, tucked into a crusty roll spread with a spicy mustard and a couple of crunchy gherkin pickles on the side. If you are out of breadcrumbs, substitute with crushed saltine crackers.

SIX SERVINGS

8 bacon strips
2 lbs ground beef
1 cup breadcrumbs
¾ cup milk (regular or low fat)
2 large eggs
½ cup chopped celery
½ cup chopped onion

½ cup chopped green peppers
½ cup chopped red peppers
1 cup tomato sauce, homemade or
  store-bought
½ cup diced cheddar cheese
2 teaspoons Worcestershire sauce
2 teaspoons Chef's salt (see tip on
  page 99)

Preheat the oven to 375° F. Lightly grease a 2-quart loaf pan.

Heat a skillet over medium heat. Add the bacon strips and cook until crisp. Remove from the pan and drain on paper towels.

Combine the ground beef, breadcrumbs, eggs and milk in a mixing bowl. Add the diced vegetables and remaining ingredients. Crumble the bacon over the mixture and combine until well blended.

Spoon the mixture into the prepared baking dish and bake for 45 minutes or until the internal temperature reaches 165° F. Remove from the oven and let rest for 10 minutes. Unmold and cut into slices.

Florentine Pot Roast with Red Wine, Mushrooms and Tomatoes

TOM VALENTI

This pot roast is inspired by the Tuscan stracotto, which means "slow cooked." The sauce is a medley of pleasing fall and winter flavors and is wonderful with creamy polenta. The Tuscan-style stew can be prepared ahead and kept refrigerated for up to 3 days or frozen for up to 1 month.

SIX SERVINGS

One 2½ lb eye round roast, excess fat trimmed and tied
3 garlic cloves, peeled and cut into slivers
2 garlic cloves, smashed and peeled
Coarse salt to taste
Freshly ground black pepper to taste
½ cup olive oil
½ lb slab bacon, cut into ½-inch strips
2 medium onions, quartered
2 celery stalks, cut crosswise into ¼-inch pieces
1 large carrot, cut crosswise into ¼-inch pieces
¼ cup tomato paste
Pinch of sugar
2 cups red wine, more if needed
1 cup dried porcini mushrooms, rinsed
One 28 oz can plum tomatoes, drained and squeezed to extract excess moisture
Handful fresh oregano leaves

Preheat the oven to 300° F.

Using a sharp thin bladed knife, make ½-inch deep slits all over the roast; insert the garlic slivers into each slit. Season the roast generously with salt and pepper.

Heat the oil in a large, heavy oven-proof pot over medium-high heat until hot but not smoking. Sear the roast on all sides until well browned, about 4 minutes per side. Remove from the pot and set aside.

Discard all but 2 tablespoons fat and add the bacon, onions, carrot and celery and cook until soft, about 5 minutes. Stir in the tomato paste and sugar.

Add the wine and 1 cup water; raise the heat to high and reduce the liquid by ½, about 5 minutes. Add the mushrooms, tomatoes and oregano, and season lightly with salt and pepper.

Return the meat to the pot. The liquid should come up to ½ to ¾; add more wine or water if necessary. Bring to a boil over high heat. Cover the pot and braise in the oven for 2 ½ to 3 hours, turning the meat over and giving the liquid a stir every ½ hour. Make sure that the liquid is simmering gently; if it's bubbling aggressively, reduce the oven temperature to 275° F.

When done, the meat will be firm to the touch and pink at the center. To serve, transfer the beef to a cutting board and slice it against the grain into 6 pieces.

Place 1 slice on each of 6 warm dinner plates. Spoon some sauce over each serving and serve the remaining sauce on the side.

Recipe adapted from Soups, Stews and One-Pot Meals. Tom Valenti and Andrew Friedman (Scribner, 2003)

TIP   This Tuscan-style stew can be prepared ahead and refrigerated for up to 3 days or frozen for up to 1 month. Defrost in the refrigerator overnight and reheat in a 300° F oven.

Sirloin Steak with Roquefort and Walnut Sauce

Although the steaks are pan-sautéed, they could also be grilled and the sauce prepared on the side in a small saucepan.

SIX SERVINGS

2 tablespoons vegetable oil
2 tablespoons butter
2 sirloin steaks, about 1 ¼ lbs each
Salt and freshly ground pepper
  to taste
1 shallot, minced

½ cup Madeira wine or red wine
⅓ cup Roquefort butter, chilled (see
  recipe page 197)
4 tablespoons toasted walnuts,
  coarsely chopped

Heat the oil and butter in a heavy skillet over high heat. Season the steaks with salt and pepper on both sides.

When the pan is very hot, add the steaks and cook for 4 to 5 minutes on each side according to the thickness of the meat and the desired doneness. Remove the steaks from the pan and let them rest for 5 to 10 minutes.

Meanwhile, discard most of the fat from the pan. Add the shallots and cook for 2 to 3 minutes over medium heat until lightly brown. Pour the Madeira or red wine into the pan, bring to a boil and reduce by ½, stirring and scraping the bottom of the pan to release any tidbits at the bottom.

Whisk the Roquefort butter into the mixture a few pieces at a time until well incorporated and blended. Stir in any juices accumulated from the resting steaks.

Slice the steaks into thick slices and divide them among 6 serving plates. Spoon the sauce over the meat slices and sprinkle with the walnuts. Serve immediately.

Tunisian Lamb Chops with Pita Bread

MINUTEMEALS CHEFS

These succulent spicy lamb chops are sautéed in a heavy cast iron skillet, but they could just as easily be cooked on a grill or campfire. Sliced tomatoes and cucumbers drizzled with olive oil, a squeeze of lemon and minced fresh mint is a refreshing counterpoint. Or try the Panzanella Salad on page 140, Warm Couscous Salad on page 137, or the Orange and Avocado Salad on page 141.

FOUR SERVINGS

8 rib lamb chops, each about 1-inch thick, trimmed

6 tablespoons olive oil

2 teaspoons ground coriander

2 teaspoons crushed dried red pepper flakes

½ teaspoon salt

4 pita breads, halved and toasted

Heat a heavy 10 to 12 inch skillet over medium heat until hot. Meanwhile, brush the lamb chops with 3 tablespoons olive oil.

In a small bowl, combine the ground coriander, crushed red pepper flakes and salt. Press the spice rub evenly onto both sides of each chop.

When the pan is hot, add the remaining olive oil. Add the chops and sauté for about 4 minutes. Turn the chops and cook for another 3 to 4 minutes until the meat is cooked to medium. Transfer the chops to a platter and serve with the toasted pita on the side.

Adapted from Minutemeals.com

Roasted Lamb Loin with Herb and Caper Sauce

This unctuous herb and caper sauce is very versatile and can be served with any type of grilled meats, fish or vegetables. It is also a great dip for crisp crudités. Serve with roasted potatoes and grilled or oven-roasted tomatoes. You may substitute the loins with a boneless leg of lamb; adjust cooking time accordingly.

FOUR SERVINGS

2 boneless lamb loins, about 1 lb each
3 tablespoons olive oil
Salt and freshly ground black pepper

HERB AND CAPER SAUCE:
1 lemon
¼ cup capers, rinsed
1 tablespoon chopped thyme
½ cup chopped parsley
1 teaspoon Dijon mustard
1 garlic clove, minced
½ cup olive oil
Freshly ground black pepper to taste

Preheat the oven to 400° F.

Season the lamb with salt and pepper on both sides. Drizzle with 1 tablespoon of olive oil and rub all over to evenly coat.

Heat the remaining olive oil in a heavy oven-proof skillet over medium-high heat. Add the loins and brown on all sides, about 5 minutes. Transfer the skillet into the oven and roast for about 10 minutes for rare, and few minutes longer for medium rare. Remove the lamb from the oven and let it rest for 5 to 10 minutes.

Meanwhile, remove two medium-size strip of the lemon rind using a vegetable peeler and set aside. Squeeze the juice.

Place the capers, thyme, parsley, mustard, lemon rind and juice, and garlic in the bowl of a food processor or blender. Process until the mixture is finely chopped. With the machine running, add the oil in a slow stream until the mixture emulsifies and thickens. Adjust seasoning with pepper to taste. Refrigerate until ready to serve.

Cut the lamb into thin slices and serve with the caper sauce on the side.

Sausage and Cabbage Stew

TOM VALENTI

This rustic stew is a speedy, pared down version of the Alsatian choucroute, a traditional dish made with many cuts of pork, fresh and smoked, buried in sauerkraut. But don't let it fool you—the flavors are as enticing and complex as the original.

SIX SERVINGS

3 tablespoons olive oil

Twelve 4 oz links sweet or spicy pork sausage or a combination, pricked with a fork

½ large Spanish onion, peeled and cut into 8 wedges

8 garlic cloves, peeled and cut into thin slivers

½ teaspoon fennel seeds

1 small Savoy cabbage, cut into 8 wedges

2 cups dry white wine

2 tablespoons distilled white vinegar

2 quarts low-sodium chicken broth or homemade

Whole-grain mustard, optional

Heat the olive oil in a large heavy-bottomed pot over medium-high heat. Add the sausages and brown all sides for 10 to 12 minutes. Remove one from the pot and cut it open to check that it is cooked all the way through to the center. The juices should run clear instead of pink and the meat should be hot all the way through the center.

Remove the sausages from the pot and set aside. Pour off all but 2 tablespoons fat from the pan.

Add the onion, garlic and fennel seeds and cook, stirring, until the onion softens but does not brown, about 4 minutes. Add the cabbage and cook for another 5 minutes.

Pour in the wine and vinegar, bring to a boil and cook until nearly completely evaporated, about 5 minutes.

Add the broth, bring to a boil over high heat, then lower the heat and simmer for 60 to 90 minutes until the flavors are well integrated and the cabbage is thoroughly softened.

Return the sausages to the pot for 15 minutes to heat through. To serve, divide the stew among 6 warm bowls and pass the mustard on the side, if desired.

Recipe adapted from Soups, Stews and One-Pot Meals. Tom Valenti and Andrew Friedman (Scribner, 2003)

Black Bean Chili

MELISSA PERELLO

Because she is a chef and cooking is one of her favorite parts of camping and because there is nothing like a satisfying meal after a full day of hiking, over the years Melissa has developed some superb grub full of sophisticated flavors. This dish is one of her favorites.

TWO TO THREE SERVINGS

1 tablespoon vegetable oil
8 oz ground beef or pork
½ cup finely minced onion
1 garlic clove, minced
¼ teaspoon chili powder
¼ teaspoon paprika
Pinch of ground cinnamon

1 large tomato, diced into ½-inch pieces
1 cup rinsed and drained black beans or ¾ cup dehydrated black beans (see note)
1 dry ancho chile pepper, seeded, rinsed and cut into thin strips

Note: These are black beans that are cooked and then dehydrated; they come in a flaky form. You can usually find them in grocery stores that sell bulk foods or most health food or organic stores.

Heat the oil in a large skillet over medium-high heat. Add the meat and brown, stirring and breaking it up into pieces with a wooden spoon. Cook thoroughly. Pour off most of the fat from the pan, leaving about 2 teaspoons.

Add the onion, garlic, spices, salt and pepper and cook over low heat until the onions are soft and translucent. Add the tomato, lower the heat to medium and cook, stirring once in a while until the liquid is reduced and mixture is almost dry. Remove from the pan and cool.

When you are ready to serve, add the beans, ancho pepper and ½ cup water to the meat mixture. Cover and simmer for 10 to 15 minutes, stirring once in a while until the beans are warm and the liquid reduced. Adjust seasoning with salt and pepper to taste.

TIP   The recipe can be prepared up to step 2. The meat mixture can then be packed into a freezer bag and held in a cooler for 2 days or frozen until ready to use.

Chili Primavera

MINUTEMEALS CHEFS

This tasty vegetarian chili takes very little time to throw together and delivers lots of big flavors. Serve it with steamed rice tossed with minced scallions and fresh herbs. Leftovers will be delicious the next morning with fried eggs and warm tortillas for a Mexican-inspired hearty breakfast.

FOUR SERVINGS

2 teaspoons olive oil
1 medium red pepper, coarsely
  chopped
1 medium onion, coarsely chopped
One 19 oz can pinto or kidney beans,
  rinsed
1 medium zucchini, thinly sliced
Two 14 ½ oz cans chili-style stewed
  tomatoes

1 cup shredded carrots
½ teaspoon salt
1 cup corn kernels, fresh or frozen
½ cup medium-spicy or hot salsa
1 cup pre-shredded Cheddar or
  Monterey Jack cheese

In a 4 to 6-quart saucepan, heat the olive oil over high heat. Add the red pepper and onion and cook, stirring occasionally, until slightly softened, about 3 minutes.

Add ½ cup water, rinsed beans, tomatoes, carrots and salt. Cover and bring the mixture to a boil. Reduce the heat to medium and simmer for 10 minutes.

Stir in the zucchini, corn and salsa and bring the chili back to a boil. Cover and reduce the heat to medium. Simmer for 5 minutes or until the vegetables are just tender.

Serve with the cheese and extra sauce on the side.

Adapted from Minutemeals.com

Maine Maple Syrup and Smokey Bacon Baked Beans

DANIEL BRUCE

A family favorite, these New England baked beans are always on the menu during the Bruce's yearly camp vacation in Maine.

EIGHT SERVINGS

1 lb Northern white beans or
  preferred dry beans
1 bottle Sam Adams Lager or
  preferred beer
½ cup molasses
½ cup maple syrup

¼ cup Dijon mustard
½ cup tomato puree
½ lb slab smoked bacon
12 pearl onions, peeled
1 teaspoon salt or more to taste
Freshly ground black pepper to taste

Place the beans in a large bowl; cover with cold water by 3 inches and soak overnight.

Preheat the oven to 325° F.

Cut the bacon into 8 large pieces. Drain the beans and place them in a heavy gauge 6-quart pot. Add the beer, molasses, syrup, mustard, tomato puree, bacon and onion. Add enough water to cover the beans, 1½ to 2 quarts depending on the size of the pot. Stir the mixture well to blend and bring to boil.

Cover and bake in the oven for 30 minutes. Stir in the salt and cook for 3 to 4 hours until the beans are tender, stirring occasionally and adding a small amount of water as necessary. Remove from the oven, adjust seasonings with salt and pepper and serve.

TIP   Baked beans may be prepared up to 3 days before serving. Gently simmer over low heat to reheat. Add 1 to 2 tablespoons of water if the mixture seems too dry.

Baked Sea Bass Papillote with Lemon and Olives

TOM VALENTI

This Mediterranean-inspired recipe can be prepared using a wide variety of fish; try snapper, striped bass, halibut, salmon, or cod. If you find yourself parked hundreds of miles away from the nearest fish shop, the sauce works equally well with skinless boneless chicken breasts; increase the oven temperature to 400° F and cook for 25 to 30 minutes. Serve with steamed baby potatoes drizzled with olive oil.

FOUR SERVINGS

2 garlic cloves, thinly sliced
2 tablespoons chopped fresh
  tarragon leaves
1 lemon, peeled and separated into
  segments
2 cups pitted olives such as Nicoise,
  Kalamata or Picholine or any
  combination

2 tablespoons chopped fresh chives
¼ cup olive oil
¼ cup dry white wine
¼ cup bottled clam juice
Salt and freshly ground black
  pepper to taste

Preheat the oven to 325° F.

Cut four 12 x 16-inch pieces of aluminum foil. Scatter the garlic, tarragon, lemon segments, olives and chives at the center of each rectangle. Drizzle with the olive oil, wine and clam juice.

Rinse and dry the fish fillets and season with salt and pepper on both sides. Place on top of the herbs and olives. Fold the foil over each fillet and tightly crimp the edges to seal the packets. Place the papillotes on a baking sheet and bake until puffed and the fish is cooked through, about 20 minutes.

Remove from the oven and transfer the papillotes to 4 serving plates; with a knife, carefully slit top of each packet and tear it to expose the fish. Serve immediately.

Recipe adapted from Soups, Stews and One-Pot Meals. Tom Valenti and Andrew Friedman (Scribner, 2003)

Pan-Fried Trout or Catch-of-the-Day with Chili and Lime

ZAK PELACCIO

Here is a spicy, exotic take on the customary campfire trout. This preparation and sauce works well with any fish filets. And of course, you don't have to be a fisherman to enjoy it.

FOUR SERVINGS

1 cup instant couscous
1 tablespoon butter
4 boned whole trout, about 10 oz each, or other fresh catch-of-the-day
Salt and freshly ground pepper to taste
Flour for dredging
6 tablespoons peanut or canola oil
1 teaspoon sugar

2 garlic cloves, minced
4 to 5 Thai, Bird's Eye or Serrano chiles, seeded and thinly sliced, or to taste
Juice of 3 to 4 limes, about ½ cup
¼ cup cilantro leaves for garnish
2 tablespoons minced fresh mint (optional)

Cook couscous according to package directions using either water or chicken broth and the 1 tablespoon butter.

Rinse and dry the fish. Season thoroughly inside and out with salt and pepper and dredge in flour, shaking off the excess.

Heat a large frying pan over high heat until it begins to smoke slightly. Add the oil to thinly coat the entire bottom of the pan. Heat for 20 seconds and add the trout. After about 30 seconds, lower the heat to medium-high. Sauté the trout for 5 minutes on each side or until golden brown and cooked through. Remove from the pan and drain on paper towels.

Discard the oil from the pan; add 1 cup water and bring to a boil, scraping the bottom of the pan to release any cooking particles. Add the sugar, garlic, sliced chiles and lime juice. Simmer for 1 to 2 minutes until sugar is dissolved.

Arrange the trout on serving plates and spoon the lime sauce over it. Garnish with the cilantro leaves. Fluff the couscous and toss in the minced mint (optional) and serve on the side.

Cod and Prosciutto Gratin

GUY MICHAUD

This is a simple super-easy one pot meal that can be enjoyed all year. Tender greens dressed in a lemony vinaigrette are all that are needed to round out the meal.

TWO SERVINGS

3 tablespoons olive oil

One 19 oz can white beans, drained and rinsed

1 tablespoon minced fresh thyme

1 tablespoon minced fresh oregano

¼ cup finely diced country ham

1 cup arugula or baby spinach leaves

½ cup chicken or vegetable broth or water

Salt and freshly ground pepper to taste

Two 7 oz cod filets, about 1-inch thick

2 slices prosciutto

Juice of ½ lemon or to taste

3 basil leaves, finely shredded

Preheat the oven to 400° F.

Lightly rub the bottom and sides of a small gratin dish with olive oil. Combine the beans, herbs, ham and arugula in the dish. Season with salt and pepper to taste and toss in the broth or water.

Rinse and dry the cod filets and place on top of the bean mixture. Cover each piece of cod with a slice of prosciutto. Drizzle with lemon juice and remaining olive oil and roast for 10 to 12 minutes, depending on the thickness of the filets, until the fish is flaky and the prosciutto crisp.

Garnish with the shredded basil and serve immediately.

Clambake

LAURENT TOURONDEL

Okay, we agree! This is not your average campsite fare but, really, clambake started along the New England shores with seafood and sausages, potatoes and corn slow-cooked over a fire dug into the sand. We are not too far off! If you find yourself within the vicinity of a good fish store, pick up the makings for this exquisite stove-top version of the Yankee classic. If you feel squeamish about splitting live lobsters, ask your fishmonger to do it as long as you promise to run back and start cooking; otherwise pick a 1-pounder per person and proceed with the recipe.

SIX SERVINGS

2 handfuls of seaweed (available in
    fish stores)
6 ears of corn, shucked, cut into
    4 pieces each
6 red potatoes, cooked until just
    tender and quartered
Three 1 ½ lb lobsters, split in half
24 littleneck clams, soaked and
    scrubbed
1 ½ cups dry white wine
6 bay leaves

In a large stock pot, arrange the seaweed evenly across the bottom. On top of the seaweed, place in layers the corn, potatoes, lobster pieces, then the clams and bay leaves.

Pour the wine into the pot. Cover the pot with a tight fitting lid, and cook over medium heat for 20 to 30 minutes.

Once the clams have opened and the lobster is fully cooked, remove from the heat. Divide the seafood and vegetables equally amongst 6 large, shallow bowls.

Spoon the cooking liquid over the top and serve immediately.

TIP For a festive presentation, assemble the clambake in individual aluminum pouches and cook them on a grill: cut twelve 14-inch long pieces of aluminum foil. Lay 2 pieces of foil on top of each other to create 6 double layered aluminum squares. Place a handful of seaweed at the center of each square. Top with 4 corn pieces, 1 red potato, ½ lobster, 4 clams and 1 bay leaf and add ¼ of the wine. Fold the foil up on all 4 sides and seal well. With a fork, poke holes in the top of each packages to allow the steam to escape. Place the packages on a medium heat and cover the grill. Cook for 20 to 30 minutes. Remove from the grill, open the packages and serve.

THRILLIN' Grillings

10 Tips to Successful Grilling and Barbecuing

1. Create a powerful, even source of heat before adding the food. Gas grills should be preheated to about 600-800° F. For charcoal grills, pile the charcoal on one side of the grill, allowing it to become about 80% white, then spread evenly.

2. Never use a fork as it punctures the meat and allows the juices to run out. Instead, use long-handled tongs and spatulas. Other useful tools include: paintbrushes for basting, wire brushes to clean the grate before adding the food and a dishtowel soaked with vegetable oil to grease the grate. Disposable foil pans and shallow pie plates are great for easy removal of meats and vegetables.

3. Use wood charcoal instead of self-starting briquettes. They give out a chemical smell that permeates the food.

4. Wood chips such as apple, hickory or mesquite, even pecan shells, add smokiness and depth of flavors to the ingredients. Just soak them in water for 15 minutes before adding to the grill.

5. Remember some foods take longer to cook than others. Plan accordingly.

6. Meats and fish should be turned only once. And don't press down! It won't cook faster, only dry out the food.

7. Check for doneness by gently poking the meat with your fingertips. A rare steak will feel like the palm of your hand between the index and the thumb, medium-rare will have a sight resilience like the bottom of the thumb and well-done will feel like the center of your hand.

8. Let the meat rest for about 10 minutes before cutting to ensure juiciness.

9. Be creative with the marinades, rubs and spice mixtures. That's half the fun of barbecuing.

10. Serve the grilled foods with store-bought or homemade condiments such as ketchups, hot salsa and sweet relishes or some of the chefs' sauces featured in this book.

—Frank Ottomanelli

Grilled Lemongrass Chicken

CYNTHIA KELLER

Lemongrass is usually available in upscale supermarkets and Asian grocery stores. If not available, substitute with grated lemon zest. Cynthia recommends serving this dish with her Curried Basmati Rice on page 130.

FOUR SERVINGS

1 stalk lemongrass, outer leaves removed and trimmed
1-inch piece of fresh ginger root, peeled
1 teaspoon sugar

2 tablespoons soy sauce
1 pinch hot pepper flakes
4 boneless, skinless chicken breasts, about 6 oz each

Using a fine grater, grate the white part of the lemongrass (beginning at the root end) and ginger into a small bowl. Stir in the sugar, soy sauce and pepper flakes and blend into a paste.

Spoon the paste over the chicken breasts and rub to evenly coat on both sides. Cover and refrigerate for at least 1 hour or overnight.

Preheat the grill to high.

Oil the grill and then place the chicken breasts on the grill. Grill for 5 minutes without moving the breasts. Turn on the other side and cook for another 4 to 5 minutes.

Remove from the grill and let the breasts rest loosely covered for 5 minutes. Slice and serve with the curried basmati rice.

Stuffed Turkey Cutlets

CHARLIE PALMER

This dish is a great way to celebrate Thanksgiving on the road! If you don't have fresh herbs on hand, you can substitute dry in the recipe; just cut the amount to 1 teaspoon each. This stuffing recipe also works wonders with boneless chicken breasts, pork cutlets as well as thick fish filets.

FOUR SERVINGS

2 tablespoons olive oil
½ cup finely chopped onions
3 tablespoons minced celery
1 ½ cups fresh white bread crumbs
1 tablespoon chopped flat leaf parsley
1 tablespoon chopped fresh tarragon leaves

1 tablespoon chopped fresh chives
Approx ¼ cup chicken broth
Coarse salt and freshly ground pepper to taste
Four 6 oz turkey cutlets at least ¾-inch thick

Place 2 teaspoons olive oil in a medium frying pan over medium heat (either stove top or grill). Add the onions and celery and cook, stirring frequently, for about 5 minutes or until just tender. Remove from the heat and stir in the bread crumbs and herbs. Add just enough chicken broth to moisten lightly, taking care not to let the mixture get wet and soggy. Season with salt and pepper to taste.

Preheat the grill to low.

Using a sharp knife, cut a pocket crosswise into the center of each turkey cutlet. Do not cut through to the opposite side as you want a closed pocket to hold the stuffing. Using your hands, neatly pack an equal portion of the stuffing into each pocket. Using toothpicks, carefully close the pocket.

Lightly coat the outside of each stuffed cutlet with some of the remaining olive oil. Season with salt and pepper to taste.

Oil the grill and then place the stuffed cutlets on it. Grill over a low heat, turning occasionally, for about 30 minutes or until the meat is cooked through and the stuffing is hot. Serve hot or at room temperature.

Chef
Charlie Palmer

CHEF, RESTAURATEUR AND
CULINARY ENTREPRENEUR

Catch Him If You Can

From coast to coast, Charlie reigns over ten establishments from fine dining to steakhouses and bistros. When not tending the stove at one of them, he is on an airplane.

Leading the Pack

His signature "Progressive American" cooking reinterprets classic European cuisine using American artisanal products and meat and produce from small farms. There is nothing quaint or dainty coming out of his kitchens; like his personality, his style is big, engaging and complex.

What a Football Player and Chef Have in Common

Charlie was a high school football star, and many expected him to go pro. Instead, he chose the Culinary Institute of America. Any regrets? No, says the former player. "In addition to the opportunity for greater career longevity and few injuries on the 'field,' as a chef I'm guaranteed access to the best ingredients and terrific meals on the road when I'm working. And I'm lucky enough to have a kitchen team equivalent to Eli Manning, Plaxico Burris and Tiki Barber."

Happy Trails

During his youth, Charlie took yearly summer RV trips with his family up to the Finger Lakes and Lake Ontario in upstate New York. Today, when his schedule permits, he prefers tent camping with his four boys while on fishing expeditions to the Bodega Bay in Northern California.

In His Coolers, You'll Find:

Small containers of sea salt, black pepper, sugar and Wonder flour for quick sautéing. Homemade croutons, assorted homemade spice rubs, thick slices of ham … and a couple of steaks just in case the fish don't take the bait.

Book Stash:

The Art of Aureole. Charlie Palmer (Ten Speed, 2003).

Great American Food. Charlie Palmer (Ten Speed, 2003).

Charlie Palmer's Casual Cooking: The Chef of New York's Aureole Restaurant Cooks for Family and Friends. Charlie Palmer (Morrow Cookbooks, 2001).

Website: WWW.CHARLIEPALMER.COM

Aureole
Mandalay Bay Resort & Casino
3950 Las Vegas Blvd. S
Las Vegas, NV 89119
702-632-7401

34 E. 61st Street
New York, NY 10021
212-319-1660

Charlie Palmer Steak
101 Constitution Ave NW
Washington, DC 20001
202-547-8100

Four Seasons Hotel
3960 Las Vegas Blvd. S
Las Vegas, NV 89119
702-632-5120

Dry Creek Kitchen
317 Healdsburg Avenue
Healdsburg, CA 95448
707-431-0330

Kitchen 22
36 E. 22nd Street
New York, NY 10017
212-228-4399

Metrazur
Grand Central Terminal, East Balcony
New York, NY 10017
212-687-4600

Quick Grilled Chicken Breasts with Summer Vegetable Salsa

JAMIE RORABACK

This colorful grilled vegetable salsa is the perfect foil for thinly pounded chicken breasts. You may want to consider making a double batch of the salsa and serve the leftovers the next day tossed with hot bowtie pasta, diced fresh tomatoes and capers.

FOUR SERVINGS

1 red or yellow pepper, seeded and quartered

1 small zucchini, cut lengthwise into ½-inch slices

1 small yellow squash, cut lengthwise into ½-inch slices

1 small red onion, cut into ½-inch slices

¼ cup plus 2 tablespoons olive oil

4 tablespoons fresh basil, coarsely chopped

2 tablespoons white balsamic vinegar or regular balsamic vinegar

4 boneless, skinless chicken breasts

Salt and freshly ground black pepper to taste

Preheat the grill to high.

Combine the pepper, zucchini, yellow squash and red onion in a mixing bowl and toss with ¼ cup olive oil.

Grill the vegetables for about 3 minutes on each side or until just tender. Remove to a cutting board and chop into a ½-inch dice. Place into a bowl and stir in the chopped basil and balsamic vinegar. Season with salt and pepper to taste and set aside at room temperature.

Place the chicken breasts on a cutting board and, using a mallet or a small heavy sauce pan, pound the breast to about ½-inch thick. Lightly coat the chicken breasts with the remaining olive oil and season to taste with salt and black pepper.

Grill the chicken breasts for 3 to 4 minutes on each side or until cooked through.

Remove the chicken from the grill and let it rest for 5 minutes. Divide the grilled vegetables among 4 serving plates and top with a chicken breast. Serve immediately.

Grilled Honey-Balsamic Marinated Quail

LAURENT TOURONDEL

Laurent suggests serving these succulent quail on their own as a snack or with lightly dressed salad greens tossed with crumbled feta or goat cheese, along with a few honey-roasted walnuts and fresh figs. Of course, roasted potatoes and grilled vegetables wouldn't be bad either.

FOUR SERVINGS

8 boneless quail (see note)
½ cup honey
½ cup balsamic vinegar
Salt and freshly ground pepper
    to taste

Note: Quail can be purchased online at www.dartagnan.com.

Butterfly the quail and thread a skewer from the bottom of the leg to the top of the breast on each side.

Combine the honey and vinegar in a shallow dish large enough to hold the quail in 1 layer. Add the quail and coat with the marinade on both sides. Refrigerate for 1 ½ hours.

Preheat the grill to medium-high.

Remove the quail from the marinade and pat dry. Pour the marinade in a small pot and reduce over medium heat by about ¼.

Season the quail with salt and pepper on both sides. Grill for about 4 to 6 minutes on each side, basting with the reduced glaze until they are nicely brown and glazed. Remove from the grill and serve hot or at room temperature.

Chef
Laurent Tourondel

CHEF/OWNER
BLT Restaurants in New York City

What's in the Name BLT

No, this is not a sandwich shop. The name stands for Bistro Laurent Tourondel, three stylish single subject eateries in New York City: BLT Fish, BLT Prime and BLT Steak. Each has its own singular identity and atmosphere but they all share Laurent's deft hand at creating simple food impeccably prepared using the finest ingredients.

A Globe-trotter at Heart

Fresh out of cooking school, Laurent's curious spirit took him to faraway destinations, from Moscow to London and eventually to New York. After Cello, the restaurant in Manhattan that made critics take notice of his young talent, closed, the chef embarked on a year-long journey through Asia, South America and Africa discovering and learning about other cultures through their food. Upon returning to the States, he was ready to take on new challenges.

RV Parks, French Style

As a child and early teen, Laurent vacationed with his family at one of the many RV parks along the Mediterranean coast of Southern France. Although he comes from a family of great home cooks, food was only the secondary focus on those vacations after beach fun and water sports. But one favorite activity was picking up fresh sardines in the early morning from small fishing boats brimming with their night catch. The silvery fish would soon end up on the grill.

Open Roads Today

Well, to tell the truth, Laurent is no longer a camper. Scurrying around the globe either for pleasure or consulting, this chef got very attached to five-star hotel room service!

So, What is He Doing in This Book?

Laurent's home cooking is unfussy and to the point. His recipes, whether for the indoor kitchen or the grill are accessible and easy to follow. They don't require too many ingredients yet deliver interesting, sophisticated flavors.

Current Journeys

For now, he is shuttling between his swanky uptown and downtown bistros in Manhattan. However, expect to see BLT's offspring sprouting around the country in the near future.

Book Stash:

Go Fish: Fresh Ideas for American Seafood.
Laurent Tourondel & Andrew Friedman (John Wiley & Sons, 2004).

BLT Steak

106 East 57th Street
New York, NY 10022
212-752-7470
WWW.BLTSTEAK.COM

BLT Fish

21 West 17th Street
New York, NY 10011
212-691-8888
WWW.BLTFISH.COM

BLT Prime

111 East 22nd Street
New York, NY 10010
212-995-8500
WWW.BLTPRIME.COM

Duck Breasts with Jack Daniel's Béarnaise

ARIANE DAGUIN

Some of the best recipes often stem from a mistake or out of desperation. A few years ago, Ariane Daguin, owner of D'Artagnan, a national purveyor of organic meats and game in this country, found herself with a freshly caught trout during a white water rafting expedition. On her way back to the camp, she was carefully mapping out her recipe of grilled trout with an unctuous Béarnaise sauce. Upon arrival, she quickly discovered that the wine supply had vanished. Rummaging through the depleted cooler, she reached for the nearest bottle—and that's how the Jack Daniel's Béarnaise was born. Try it like the original with a trout or, as in this recipe, with duck breasts or grilled steaks. Serve with Charlie's Savory Potatoes on the Grill on page 152.

FOUR SERVINGS

16 tablespoons unsalted butter
½ cup Jack Daniel's whiskey
1 tablespoon wine vinegar
1 tablespoon minced shallots
1 tablespoon dried tarragon
Salt and freshly ground pepper
  to taste

3 egg yolks
2 tablespoons minced fresh tarragon
  or any fresh herb available
2 duck magrets, about 1 lb each
  (see note)

Note: Magret, the breast of moulard ducks, is available in most upscale supermarkets or can be purchased online at www.dartagnan.com. Each breast weighs about 1 lb and yields 2 servings. If not available, substitute with regular duck breast; select 1 per person.

Preheat the grill to medium-hot.

In a heavy-based saucepan, melt the butter. Simmer it until the water evaporates and the milk solids settle on the bottom of the pan. Remove from the heat and let the melted butter sit for a few minutes so any remaining solids fall to the bottom. Skim off the foam on top.

In a small saucepan combine the whiskey, vinegar, shallots and dried tarragon and simmer over moderate heat until reduced to about 2 tablespoons.

In a mixing bowl, whisk the egg yolks until they thicken. Strain the reduced Jack Daniel's and vinegar over the yolks and whisk to combine. Place the bowl over a saucepan of simmering, not boiling, water. Whisk until mixture is warm and thick, about 2 minutes. Remove the bowl from the heat.

Add the melted butter to the egg mixture, 1 tablespoon at a time, whisking thoroughly to incorporate before each addition. As the mixture begins to thicken and becomes creamy, the butter can be added more rapidly. Do not add the milk solids at the bottom of the melted butter. Season the sauce to taste with the fresh tarragon or herbs, salt and pepper. Keep warm.

Meanwhile, score the skin of the duck breasts and season with salt and pepper. Place the breasts skin side down on the grill and cook for 10 minutes, moving them around as the dripping fat flares up. Turn the breasts and grill another 5 minutes. The breasts are best cooked medium rare.

Remove the breasts from the grill and let them rest for 5 minutes. Cut into ½-inch slices and divide them among 4 serving plates. Serve immediately with the Béarnaise sauce on the side.

TIP   For the purists, here is the recipe for the classic Béarnaise sauce.

16 tablespoons unsalted butter
½ cup dry white wine
1 tablespoon wine vinegar
1 tablespoon minced shallots
2 tablespoons minced fresh tarragon,
   plus 1 teaspoon for garnish

Salt and freshly ground pepper
   to taste
3 egg yolks
1 teaspoon freshly squeezed lemon
   juice

Proceed with the recipe. Whisk in the lemon juice and 1 teaspoon tarragon at the end.

Grilled Chicken and Andouille Sausage Kabobs in Flour Tortillas

JIMMY BANNOS

You can serve these delicious kabobs as wrap sandwiches for a quick spicy meal. You can also omit the tortillas and serve them as a main course with the Barbecue Sweet Corn (on page 152), Quick Ratatouille (on page 154) or the Orange and Avocado Salad (on page 141).

FOUR SERVINGS

8 skewers
1 lb boneless, skinless chicken
   breasts, cut into 1-inch cubes
8 oz andouille sausage, cut into 16
   slices
1 ½ teaspoons Creole seasoning
      (see note)

1 tablespoon olive oil
¼ teaspoon black pepper
8 flour tortillas
Spicy mustard to taste

Note: Creole seasoning is a spice blend available in most supermarkets. There are many varieties but it usually includes cayenne pepper, paprika and dried herbs such as garlic, thyme and oregano.

Soak the bamboo skewers in cold water for 1 hour before using. This is to keep them from catching fire when placed over the hot fire.

Preheat the grill to high. Brush and oil the grate.

Alternately thread the chicken pieces and 2 pieces andouille onto each skewer. Place on a flat plate. Drizzle the olive oil over the kabobs. Season each kabob with the Creole seasoning and black pepper.

Grill the kabobs, turning occasionally to ensure even cooking, for about 6 to 8 minutes. Grill the tortillas for 1 to 2 minutes on each side until just toasted and warm.

Remove from the grill and spread with mustard. Slide the chicken and sausage off each skewer onto a tortilla. Roll up and serve immediately.

Grilled Steak with Caramelized Onion and Goat Cheese

CHEF HARRY

Serve these steaks with a side of Grilled Asparagus (page 154) and Brussels Sprouts and Potatoes en Papillote (page 155).

FOUR SERVINGS

4 tablespoons butter
1 medium onion, thinly sliced
1 teaspoon sugar
2 tablespoons extra-dry Vermouth

2 shell steaks, about 12 oz each
1 cup crumbled goat cheese
Salt and freshly ground pepper
   to taste

Preheat the grill to medium-hot.

Melt the butter in a skillet over medium-high heat, add the onion and sauté for 5 minutes or until soft and translucent.

Reduce the heat to medium-low and sprinkle the sugar and vermouth over the onions. Continue cooking, stirring once in a while until the onion is very soft and turns caramel in color. Keep warm.

Generously season the steaks with salt and pepper on both sides. Place the steaks on the grill and cook for 5 minutes without moving. Turn on the other side and grill to taste. Transfer to a serving platter and let steaks rest for 5 to 10 minutes. Top the steaks with the onions and the goat cheese and serve.

TIP   The warm caramelized onions and goat cheese mixture is delicious on its own. You really don't need a steak to enjoy it! Toast some French bread slices and serve with the mixture for a wonderful appetizer or supper! Or use it as a topping for grilled pizza (on page 112).

Malted Mole Rubbed Barbecued Hanger Steak with Fennel, Tomato, Potato Ragout

DANIEL BRUCE

This unusual spice rub mixture is loosely inspired by the Mexican mole sauce, a rich dark concoction made with chocolate and spices. Don't skip making the vegetable ragout; it is a bright complement to the intensely flavored steak.

FOUR SERVINGS

MOLE RUBBED STEAK:
¼ cup unsweetened cocoa powder
2 tablespoons honey
1 teaspoon cardamom
1 teaspoon cumin
½ tablespoon Chinese Five Spice (see note)
1 teaspoon salt
1 tablespoon hot chili paste
¼ cup Malt beer
Four 7 oz hanger steaks

VEGETABLE RAGOUT:
6 red bliss potatoes
1 small fennel bulb
2 tablespoons olive oil
2 large tomatoes, cored and cut into large dice
Salt and freshly ground pepper to taste

Note: Chinese Five Spice is a fragrant blend of ground spices that includes equal parts cinnamon, cloves, fennel, Szechuan peppercorns and star anise. It is available in Asian markets.

Combine all the ingredients for the rub in a large bowl except the steaks; mix well to form a paste. Add the hanger steaks and coat well. Refrigerate for at least 2 hours.

Preheat the grill to high.

Wash and cut the potatoes into wedges, place in a saucepan and cover with lightly salted cold water. Bring to a boil and simmer until cooked but still firm, about 10 to 15 minutes. Drain the potatoes and cool on a cookie sheet.

Cut off the green fronds from the fennel; mince them and set aside. Discard the tough outer leaves and stocks and cut the bulb into thin wedges. Heat a sauté pan over medium-high heat. Add the olive oil and sauté the fennel wedges until golden brown on both sides. Add the potatoes and tomatoes and stir to combine. Season with salt and pepper to taste and simmer for 8 to 10 minutes. Keep warm.

Remove the steaks from the marinade and grill for 6 minutes on each side for medium rare or until the desired doneness. Remove from the grill and let them rest for 5 minutes.

Cut each steak into thin slices and serve with the hot vegetable ragout. Garnish with the reserved fennel tops.

Beef Primer: What's in the Grades

The Best: **USDA Prime.** This beef has the most marbling. Prime graded beef is mostly sold to fine butcher shops and restaurants and is seldom found in grocery stores. Only 2% of all beef graded in the U.S. achieves the Prime Grade.

The 2nd Best: **USDA Choice.** This beef has a good amount of marbling but less than USDA Prime.

The 3rd Best: **USDA Select.** This one was formerly known as USDA Good. The beef is less marbled than USDA Choice. It isn't as tender, juicy or flavorful as USDA Prime or Choice.

Meat Buying Guidelines

1 Cuts of beef that are boneless and lean usually yield up to 4 servings per pound

2 Cuts of beef with some bone usually yield up to 3 servings per pound.

3 When shopping for meats, it is always better to buy extra or more than needed. Planning for larger appetites is always good. If you have leftovers, cooked beef can be stored in the refrigerator for 3 to 4 days without spoilage. There are many ways to use leftovers from sandwiches to noodle soups. Uncooked meats can be frozen.

—Frank Ottomanelli

Rib Eye Steak with Chimichurri Sauce

FRANCIS MALLMANN

An addictive spicy sauce, chimichurri is a staple at any Argentinean *asado* or barbecue, and every cook and gaucho in the country has a secret recipe. Francis's version is a piquant blend of pepper flakes, parsley and minty oregano. The sauce can be kept refrigerated for up to a week and is also delicious with grilled sausages, chicken or duck breasts. Crisp pan-roasted potatoes showered with minced garlic and parsley is all that is needed for a true Argentinean feast.

FOUR SERVINGS

2 rib eye steaks, about 14 oz each
Sea salt and freshly ground pepper to
   taste

CHIMICHURRI SAUCE:
½ cup water
½ cup olive oil
½ cup red wine vinegar
½ tablespoon red pepper flakes
½ teaspoon sea salt
½ cup minced oregano
½ cup minced parsley
4 garlic cloves, minced

To make the Chimichurri sauce: combine all the ingredients into a jar. Cover with a tight lid and shake well to combine. Let sit at room temperature for at least 2 hours before serving.

Preheat the grill to high.

Season the steaks with sea salt and pepper on both sides and place on the grill. Do not move the steaks from the place where they made first contact on the grill; this will give them the perfect crust and seal. Cook the steaks for about 6 minutes (without moving them) on the first side; flip to the other side and cook for about 3 minutes or a few minutes longer, according to the desired doneness.

Remove the meat from the grill and let it rest for 5 to 10 minutes. Thinly slice the steaks and place on a serving platter. Drizzle with some of the Chimichurri sauce and serve with the remainder on the side.

Grilled Skirt Steak

PATRICIA WILLIAMS

Orange and rosemary is an appealing combination often found in Mediterranean dishes. In this marinade, their pungent refreshing tangs play well against each other without overpowering the flavor of the steak. Be careful not to overcook the meat; it will become tough. Patricia likes to serve this tasty recipe with her panzanella salad on page 140.

FOUR SERVINGS

One 16 oz skirt steak
3 tablespoons olive oil
2 sprigs rosemary, roughly chopped
2 sprigs thyme, roughly chopped
2 garlic cloves, thinly sliced

Zest of 2 oranges, cut into
   long strips
Salt and freshly ground pepper
   to taste

Place the steak and all remaining ingredients in a large plastic bag. Seal the bag and shake to evenly distribute the seasonings and thoroughly coat the meat. Refrigerate for at least 2 hours or overnight.

When ready to serve, preheat the grill to high.

Remove the steak from the marinade and discard the garlic and herbs. Wipe off as much oil as possible from the steak.

Season the steak on both sides with salt and pepper and grill for 3 to 4 minutes on each side for medium rare. Remove the steak from the grill and let it rest for 4 to 5 minutes.

Cut into thin slices and serve with the panzanella salad.

Grilled Beef Fillets with Hominy, Peas, Corn and Truffle Butter

NEAL FRASER

Smart cooks know to keep a little jar of truffle butter hidden in the freezer of their nomadic kitchen (and their stationary one, for that matter). This deeply earthy, aromatic ingredient is one of those small luxury items which can turn the most ordinary meal into an exceptional one. In this recipe, you may substitute canned corn and peas with fresh or frozen ones.

FOUR SERVINGS

6 beef fillets, about 6 to 8 oz each
Salt and freshly ground pepper
   to taste
One 20 oz can hominy
One 15 oz can corn kernels

One 15 oz can peas
3 tablespoons butter
¾ cup chicken stock
3 oz black truffle butter, cut into six
   pieces (see note)

Note: Black or white truffle butter is available in gourmet and specialty stores. It can also be purchased online. See resource page 202.

Preheat the grill to high.

Season the fillets with salt and pepper on both sides and set aside.

Drain and rinse the hominy, corn and peas and place into a saucepan. Add the chicken broth and bring to a simmer. Season with salt and pepper to taste and cook for a couple of minutes until the vegetables are hot. Swirl in the butter and keep warm.

Place the beef fillets on the grill and cook 4 to 6 minutes on each side, according to desired doneness and thickness of the meat. Remove from the grill, top each fillet with truffle butter and let the meat rest for 5 minutes. Serve with the vegetable ragout on the side.

Spicy Turkey Burgers

MINUTEMEALS CHEFS

Ground fresh turkey meat is bland and needs to be highly seasoned before grilling or sautéing. It needs salt and pepper, of course, but also flavorings such as shallots, fresh herbs and spices. This burger has an appealing spicy Asian slant that could become quite addictive. Beware: Chinese chili paste is extremely hot and spicy; make sure to adjust the amount according to taste. Spicy mustard, available in supermarkets, is less fiery and makes a good substitute.

FOUR SERVINGS

1 ½ lbs lean ground turkey
2 tablespoons lite soy sauce
2 teaspoons toasted sesame oil
2 teaspoons Chinese chili paste with garlic or less to taste (available in Asian markets)

4 teaspoons canola oil
4 whole-grain burger buns
4 lettuce leaves
4 tomato slices
Spicy mustard and ketchup as condiments

Preheat the grill to high.

In a medium bowl, blend together the turkey, soy sauce, sesame oil and chili paste. Form the meat into 4 patties.

Grill the patties for about 5 minutes per side or until cooked through. Meanwhile, place the buns on the grill cut side down for 1 to 2 minutes until lightly toasted.

Layer each bun halve with a lettuce leaf and a slice of tomato. Top with the burgers and cover with the remaining buns. Serve with mustard and ketchup or other favorite condiments.

Adapted from Minutemeals.com

What-a-Burger

FRANK OTTOMANELLI

When the Ottomanelli clan gets together for a summer cookout, this juicy burger is often on the menu to the great pleasure of children and parents alike.

SIX SERVINGS

6 bacon strips
1 ½ lbs ground beef
½ cup grated cheddar cheese or your favorite melting cheese
2 small green peppers, seeded and cut into small dice

1 small onion, cut into small dice
2 tablespoons Worcestershire sauce
Chef's salt to taste (see tip)
6 burger buns
Ketchup, mustard and any favorite condiments for topping

Preheat the grill to hot.

Heat a skillet over medium heat. Add the bacon strips and cook until crisp. Remove from the pan and drain on paper towels.

In a mixing bowl, blend together the ground beef, diced green peppers, onion, cheese and Worcestershire sauce. Crumble the bacon over the mixture and season with chef's salt to taste. Blend until well combined. Form the meat mixture into 6 patties and set aside in a cool place until ready to grill.

Place the burgers on the grill and cook for about 4 to 5 minutes per side to the desired doneness. Meanwhile, place the burger buns cut side down on the grill for 1 to 2 minutes to toast. Remove the burgers from the grill and serve on the buns with assorted condiments and chef's salt on the side.

TIP   Keep this chef's salt handy—it is a fine seasoning for grilled or roasted meats.

2 tablespoons salt
1 tablespoon freshly ground pepper

1 tablespoon paprika
1 tablespoon garlic powder

Combine all the ingredients in a small jar or sealable plastic bag. Store in a dry place until ready to use.

Blue Cheese Burgers

MINUTEMEALS CHEFS

Here is a different take on the ordinary cheeseburger. Blue cheese has a singular affinity with the meat patty, but you could just as easily sneak in any soft melting cheese cut into small slices—Brie, mozzarella, Swiss, Cheddar or fresh goat cheese. The combinations are infinite.

FOUR SERVINGS

1 ½ lbs ground sirloin
About 1 teaspoon each of salt and
  freshly ground black pepper
4 to 6 oz blue cheese or Roquefort at
  room temperature

4 large burger buns
Sliced tomatoes, sliced onions,
  lettuce leaves, ketchup, mustard
  and any favorite condiments for
  topping and garnish.

Preheat the grill to medium.

Break up the sirloin and season with the salt and pepper. Divide the meat equally into 4 mounds. Halve the mounds and flatten each ½ into patties about ¼-inch thick.

Quarter the blue cheese and roll each piece into a ball. Flatten each ball into a disk about the size of a 50-cent coin. Place a disk of cheese at the center of each patty, making sure to leave a ¼-inch edge all the way around. Top with the remaining patties. Flatten each burger gently between the palms of your hands, then pinch the edge of the 2 patties together firmly to seal and enclose the cheese.

Place the burgers on the grill, and cook for about 4 to 5 minutes per side to the desired doneness. Meanwhile, place the burger buns cut side down on the grill for 1 to 2 minutes to toast.

Remove the burgers from the grill and serve on the buns with assorted condiments and garnishes.

Adapted from Minutemeals.com

Veal Hanger Steak and Vegetable Skewers

LAURENT TOURONDEL

Veal hanger steak is a cut of meat that is slowly making its debut on restaurant menus around the country. Its texture is tender and the flavor more delicate than beef hanger steak. Use the latter if you can't convince your butcher to secure this coveted cut. The spice rub can be used on veal, beef or poultry.

SIX SERVINGS

12 long wooden skewers, soaked in water

12 veal or beef hanger steaks, cut into 48 pieces approx 1 x 1-inch

12 button mushrooms, trimmed

12 cherry tomatoes

1 zucchini, cut into 12 pieces, approx 1 x 1-inch

1 onion, cut into pieces, approx 1 x 1-inch

1 red pepper, cut into 12 square pieces, approx 1 x 1-inch

¼ cup olive oil

Fine sea salt and freshly ground black pepper to taste

SPICE RUB:

1 tablespoon paprika

1 ½ tablespoons dried oregano

1 tablespoon coarsely ground black pepper

1 tablespoon fine sea salt

1 ½ tablespoons dried thyme

1 tablespoon sugar

2 tablespoons garlic powder

Preheat the grill to medium.

Combine the ingredients for the spice rub in a small bowl. Sprinkle the cubed veal or beef with the mixture and toss to coat evenly.

To assemble the skewers: thread a piece of onion on a skewer, add a piece of veal or beef, a cherry tomato, another piece of meat, zucchini, meat, mushrooms, meat and red pepper. Repeat with each skewer. Season the skewers with salt and pepper, drizzle with the olive oil and grill for about 3 minutes on each side. Serve immediately.

TIP Measure out and pack the spice blend in a small plastic bag or container before you leave. The blend can also be used as a rub on poultry or as a seasoning for sautéed vegetables. Don't forget to label it.

"Flipped & Flapped" Lamb Steaks and Griddle Potatoes

FRANCIS MALLMANN

This recipe is the perfect example of the "flipped and flapped" technique Francis has developed over the years. Yes, it is somewhat involved with three different elements—the lamb, potatoes and tomato salad. And, yes, each one is delicious on its own. But what makes this recipe enticing and rewarding as a whole are its many layers of textures and flavors.

SIX TO EIGHT SERVINGS

3 to 4 lbs boneless, butterfly leg of lamb
Salt and freshly ground pepper to taste
1 cup extra-strong Dijon mustard
½ cup olive oil
½ cup minced thyme leaves

GRIDDLE POTATOES:
6 unpeeled medium potatoes
2 tablespoons red wine vinegar or to taste
6 tablespoons olive oil

TOMATO SALAD:
3 cups cherry tomatoes, halved
1 small red onion, thinly sliced
1 cup chopped parsley
1 tablespoon mustard
3 tablespoons good-quality red wine vinegar
½ cup olive oil
Salt and freshly ground pepper to taste
1 cup sliced toasted almonds

Cut the potatoes into big chunks and cook in lightly salted water until tender, about 15 minutes. Drain in a colander and cool.

When cool enough to handle, coarsely crush the potatoes with your hands or a potato masher. Season to taste with the vinegar, 3 tablespoons olive oil, salt and pepper. Set aside.

Trim the leg of lamb and discard any fat and gristle. Cut against the grain into 1-inch slices. Using a mallet or a small heavy saucepan, pound each slice to ½-inch thick. Season with salt and pepper on both sides.

Combine the mustard and thyme and spread the mixture on both sides of each lamb steak. Set aside.

Combine the cherry tomatoes, sliced red onions and parsley in a bowl. Whisk together the mustard, vinegar, salt and pepper in a mixing bowl. Slowly add the olive oil, whisking constantly until the mixture is smooth and emulsified. Toss with the tomato salad and set aside.

When ready to cook, preheat the grill to high.

Place 2 large heavy skillets or cast iron skillets on the grate of the grill and heat as hot as you can. Add the mustard coated lamb in one of the skillets and cook without moving the meat for 3 minutes. Flip the lamb steaks and cook for 2 minutes longer.

Add the remaining 3 tablespoons olive oil to the other hot skillet. Spread the crushed potatoes in an even layer. The potatoes should fit comfortably, not squeezed into the pan. Cook until the bottom is crisp and golden brown.

Remove from the skillet and carefully slide onto a serving dish. Sprinkle with the toasted almonds and top with the tomato salad. Serve immediately with the mustard lamb.

Chef
Francis Mallmann

Globe-trotting, South American Style

Francis Mallmann is a chef, restaurant owner, international consultant, special events wizard and TV personality. Oh, and did we mention that his restaurants are in Uruguay and Argentina and his consulting in the United States and Europe?

When Does He Find Time to RV?

Unfortunately, never. This type of recreational pastime is not part of the South American lifestyle—not yet, anyway. But Francis escapes to faraway places, especially to his log cabin on a nearly deserted island in Patagonia. Getting there is a 500-mile car trek through rough mountainous terrain, ending with a 25-mile boat ride across a lake.

So, What is He Doing in This Book?

Francis is a master at "cooking with fire" and his imagination knows no bounds. After spending a few years in the kitchens of France's most extraordinary chefs, Francis couldn't wait to go home and emulate his masters. Soon he was deemed Argentina's best chef. A decade ago, the genial chef decided to go back to his culinary roots and simplicity and grilling is a big part of the equation.

Blazing Trails

Going further in his renewed interest in indigenous cooking, Francis is currently developing and hosting a series for the Discovery Channel, a journey along the 5000-mile trail at the foot of the Andes, exploring the many cultures, people and various open fire cooking techniques along the way.

Flip Flapping

He has spent a lot of time observing and learning the indigenous cooking methods of the Andes, from baking empanadas and breads in clay ovens to the lesser known *infiernillo* or "Little Hell." This is a method used by the Incas in which food is wedged between two wood fires on different sized iron griddles. Could this be the precursor to the broiler? But his current favorite technique is what he calls "flipped & flapped." A cast-iron pan is heated until very hot on an open fire and the food is flash-cooked and almost charred on one side before flipping it to the other side. Meats pounded very thin are delicious cooked this way. So are vegetables such as parboiled potatoes, carrots, asparagus, squash or very ripe tomato slices. However, fish, he maintains, should receive much gentler treatment.

Patagonia Sur

Rocha 803
La Boca
Buenos Aires, Argentina

Francis Mallmann 1884

Belgrano 1188
Mendoza, Patagonia
WWW.ESCORIHUELA.COM.AR

Garzon Hotel & Restaurante

Garzon, Uruzay
WWW.RESTAURANTGARZON.COM

Los Negros

Calle de Los Teros Junto al Faro de José Ignacio
Punta Del Este, Uruguay

Pork Chops with Vietnamese Glaze and Shredded Carrot Salad

ZAK PELACCIO

This recipe is inspired by the traditional Vietnamese marinated BBQ pork. As a variation, toss finely shredded lettuce or cabbage, or blanched and sliced green beans into the carrot salad. Adjust the amount of dressing accordingly.

FOUR SERVINGS

3 tablespoons sugar
¼ cup rice vinegar
3 tablespoons fish sauce (nuoc mam) or lite soy sauce
1 jalapeño pepper, seeded and minced (if not available use ½ teaspoon red pepper flakes)
2 garlic cloves, minced
4 scallions, minced
4 double-cut pork chops or 8 thin sliced pork chops

CARROT SALAD:
1 lb carrots, peeled and finely shredded
4 tablespoons minced mint leaves
3 tablespoons minced cilantro
2 to 3 tablespoons fish sauce or lite soy sauce to taste
2 tablespoons rice vinegar or red wine vinegar
¼ cup olive oil
½ teaspoon dried chili flakes
1 tablespoon sugar
Juice of 1 lime or more to taste

Combine the sugar, vinegar, fish sauce, pepper, garlic and scallions in a large mixing bowl. Stir to dissolve the sugar. Add the pork chops and coat with the mixture on all sides. Marinate in a refrigerator for at least 1 hour.

Preheat the grill to medium-high.

Combine the carrots and minced herbs in a serving bowl. In a mixing bowl, whisk together the sugar, vinegar, fish sauce, olive oil, chili flakes and lime juice until well combined and the sugar is dissolved. Add to the carrots and toss. Adjust the seasonings to taste with salt and more lime juice, if desired.

Grill the pork chops for 8 to 10 minutes (less if using thin chops) on each side, depending on the thickness of the chops. Place pork chops on serving plates and serve with the carrot salad on the side.

Watermelon-Cranberry Glazed Pork Chops

CHEF HARRY

Keep Chef Harry's watermelon-cranberry glaze recipe handy when the holiday season comes around. It will make a pleasant and novel accompaniment to the traditional roast turkey or ham.

EIGHT SERVINGS

8 pork chops, about 7 oz each
2 cups pineapple juice
½ cup soy sauce
1 tablespoon rosemary leaves
3 garlic cloves, minced
1 tablespoon cracked black pepper

WATERMELON-CRANBERRY GLAZE:
2 cups watermelon puree
4 cups fresh or frozen cranberries
1 cup sugar
A dash of ground clove
½ teaspoon cinnamon

Place the pork chops, pineapple juice, soy sauce, rosemary, garlic and pepper in a large sealable plastic bag. Seal the bag and shake to evenly distribute the seasonings and thoroughly coat the meat. Refrigerate for at least 2 hours or overnight.

Combine all the ingredients for the glaze in a heavy saucepan. Bring to a simmer and cook, stirring frequently for about 20 minutes or until the cranberries are soft and the sauce is thick. The glaze can be prepared ahead and refrigerated for up to 3 days.

Preheat the grill to medium-high.

Remove the chops from the bag and wipe off the garlic and rosemary leaves. Grill the chops for 6 to 8 minutes on each side or to taste.

Meanwhile, bring the glaze back to a simmer. Place the chops on a serving platter and spoon the glaze over them. Serve immediately.

TIP To puree watermelon: remove the rind and cut into chunks. Discard the seeds and place in a food processor fitted with a steel blade. Process until pureed. You may also mash it with the back of a fork and puree in a blender.

Grilled Pancetta-Wrapped Trout

PATRICIA WILLIAMS

Here is an updated version of the campfire trout wrapped in bacon that Patricia's father prepared on their yearly journey through the Salt Grass Trail in Texas. Pancetta is unsmoked Italian bacon that has been cured in salt and herbs. Thinly sliced and wrapped around the fish, it lends a delicate crispiness to the trout.

EIGHT SERVINGS

4 boned whole trout, about 10 oz each
1 lemon, thinly sliced
8 sprigs thyme
4 garlic cloves, thinly sliced

Salt and freshly ground pepper to taste
16 thin slices pancetta or bacon (see note)

Note: Pancetta is available in most supermarkets. Tightly wrapped, it can be kept refrigerated for up to 3 weeks or frozen for up to 6 months.

Preheat the grill to medium-high.

Rinse the trout under cold water and pat dry with paper towels.

Season the trout with salt and pepper. Place 2 sprigs of thyme, 1 thinly sliced garlic clove and 3 slices lemon inside each cavity. Wrap 4 pancetta (or bacon) slices around each trout, overlapping them slightly and leaving the head and tail exposed.

Place the trout on the grill and cook for 3 to 4 minutes on each side until the flesh is opaque and moist and the pancetta crisp. Remove from the grill and serve immediately.

Mediterranean Salmon Skewers

CHARLIE PALMER

This is a simple marinade that accents the sweet salmon very nicely. You could also use Charlie's Asian Marinade on page 188. Chicken or turkey breasts could be cut and cooked in this same fashion.

FOUR SERVINGS

8 bamboo skewers
Eight 1-inch thick by 4-inches long
  pieces salmon filet
¼ cup olive oil
Juice and zest of 1 lemon

1 tablespoon chopped fresh oregano,
  tarragon, chervil or dill
½ teaspoon minced garlic
Coarse salt and freshly ground
  pepper to taste

Soak the bamboo skewers in cold water for 1 hour before using. This is to keep them from catching fire when placed over the hot fire.

Preheat the grill to medium-hot. Brush and oil the grate.

Thread each piece of salmon lengthwise onto a soaked skewer.

Combine the olive oil, lemon juice and zest, herbs, garlic and salt and pepper to taste. Brush the mixture onto the salmon skewers.

Place the skewers on a medium-hot fire and grill, turning frequently, for about 8 minutes or until the fish is nicely glazed and just barely cooked through. Remove from the grill and serve immediately.

Fire Crackers

CHEF HARRY

Although these zesty bites are quite appropriate for an Independence Day celebration, they are awesome finger foods for year-round outdoor cocktail parties! Stuff a bunch of them the night before and refrigerate until the festivities begin.

MAKES 8 FIRECRACKERS

8 Anaheim chiles (see note)
6 oz soft herbed goat cheese
8 oz cooked crab meat, rinsed and
   picked over
1 garlic clove, minced

1 jalapeño pepper, seeded and
   minced
2 tablespoons mayonnaise
2 tablespoons olive oil

Note: Anaheim chile, also called California green chile, are large, mild chiles perfect for stuffing. If not available, New Mexico green chile or poblano chile, although a little hotter than the Anaheim, are good substitutes.

Preheat the grill to high.

Rinse and dry the Anaheim chiles. Slit one side of each pepper just enough to remove the seeds. Discard the seeds.

Combine the goat cheese, crab meat, garlic, jalapeño and mayonnaise and stir with a fork until well blended. Spoon the mixture into the seeded peppers.

Brush the peppers all over with the olive oil and grill, turning frequently just until the peppers begin to char and blister and the cheese begins to ooze from the slit. Remove to a platter and serve.

Portobello Reubens

MINUTEMEALS CHEFS

Portobello mushrooms are large, fleshy mushrooms available in most supermarkets. Because of their rich meaty flavor and firm texture, they are an excellent alternative to beef, especially when marinated in olive oil and fresh herbs and seared on the grill, or as in this recipe, stuffed with a savory filling. If you don't have Thousand Island dressing, make your own: stir ketchup and chopped pickle with mayonnaise, or simpler still, use chili sauce in place of the ketchup and pickle. Serve with one of the Potato Salads (page 144 and 145) and Vegetable Slaw (page 140).

EIGHT SERVINGS

4 large Portobello mushrooms, stems removed
2 tablespoons olive oil
Salt and pepper to taste

¾ cup drained organic sauerkraut
6 oz thinly sliced Swiss cheese
2 tablespoons store-bought Thousand Island dressing or to taste

Preheat the grill to medium-high.

Rinse and drain the sauerkraut. With your hands, squeeze out as much water as possible.

Brush the mushroom caps on both sides with the olive oil and season with salt and pepper. Place them open side down on the grill and cook for about 5 minutes.

Turn the mushrooms open side up. Fill each cap with some of the sauerkraut and top with the Swiss cheese slices. Cover the grill and cook for 2 to 3 minutes or until the cheese is melted and the sauerkraut is hot. Transfer each mushroom cap to a plate and spoon ½ tablespoon (or more to taste) Thousand Island dressing over each. Serve immediately.

Adapted from Minutemeals.com

Spicy Sausage Grilled Pizza

Once you have mastered the technique for grilled pizza, you'll have a hard time going back to your local pizza joint. Stretching and grilling the dough requires a little practice, but not so much that it should prevent you from trying this recipe.

This dough includes cornmeal, which gives it a pleasing texture and a rustic flavor. If the task of making your own is a little too daunting, pick some fresh dough from your local pizza place or fresh frozen dough at the supermarket. Whatever you do, do not use a pre-cooked pie shell. Either homemade or store-bought pizza dough can be frozen until ready to use. Stock your freezer with a few of them before leaving.

The suggested toppings are guidelines. You can really adjust the ingredients according to your liking or you can create your very own grilled pie with your favorite toppings. Last, grilled pizzas are great when entertaining children and adults alike. Just lay out as many ingredients already cut up or sliced as you can and let your guests go wild.

FOUR 8 TO 10-INCH INDIVIDUAL PIZZAS

BASIC PIZZA DOUGH RECIPE:
1 packet active dry yeast
1 ¼ cups warm water
½ teaspoon sugar
½ teaspoon sea salt
¼ cup cornmeal
3 tablespoons olive oil
3 ½ to 4 cups unbleached flour, plus more for dusting the board

TOPPING:
1 cup seasoned tomato pizza sauce, homemade or store-bought
½ lb cured spicy sausage such as andouille, pepperoni or chorizo, thinly sliced (see note)
2 cups grated fresh mozzarella
5 teaspoons minced fresh sage or 4 tablespoons minced basil

Note: Chorizo is a cured spicy sausage from Spain. It is available in most supermarkets or can be purchased online. (See resource page 202).

Dissolve the yeast in the warm water with the sugar in a large mixing bowl. When the yeast starts to foam, stir in the salt, cornmeal and oil. Gradually add the flour, stirring with a wooden spoon.

Place the dough on a floured work surface and knead until the dough is smooth and shiny. Add a little flour to the dough while kneading if it is sticking. Place the dough in a bowl that has been brushed with olive oil. Cover the bowl with plastic wrap or a towel and set in a warm place until doubled in bulk, about 2 hours.

Punch down the dough, knead briefly and let rise again for about 40 minutes. Divide the dough into 4 balls. Loosely cover each one and set aside for at least 1 hour or until ready to grill. At this point, you can proceed with the recipe or wrap the dough balls individually in plastic wrap and freeze until ready to use.

Preheat the grill to hot and set the grill rack 3 to 4 inches above the coals. Set out the topping ingredients.

Whether you are using store-bought or homemade dough, with your hands, stretch and flatten one of the pizza doughs into an 8 to 10 inch free-form circle, making sure not to create a thick border. The dough should be flat throughout. If the dough shrinks back, let it rest for a few minutes before spreading it out again. Make sure not to stretch the dough too thin. Repeat with the remaining dough.

Carefully place the four pizza dough onto the grill. Within 1 minute, they will puff slightly, the undersides will crisp up and grill marks will appear. Using tongs, immediately flip the crusts over onto the coolest part of the grill. Quickly spread ¼ cup tomato sauce on each grilled surface, layer ½ cup mozzarella and ¼ of the spicy sausage and sprinkle with some of the herbs. Carefully, slide the pizzas onto a medium-hot spot on the grill and continue cooking until the topping is hot and the cheese melted. Remove from the grill and serve immediately.

Suggested Toppings:

Onion and Goat Cheese: Prepare Chef Harry's caramelized onions (on page 91), using 5 onions and ¼ cup Vermouth. Spread the onion mixture onto the pizzas and dot each one with crumbled goat cheese, pitted black olives and fresh thyme leaves or shredded basil.

Pizza Bianca: Brush the grilled side of the pizzas with olive oil. Sprinkle each one with ½ teaspoon minced garlic, layer with thin slices of fresh mozzarella and sprinkle with grated Parmesan and diced fresh tomatoes. Sprinkle with shredded fresh basil just before serving.

Seafood Pizza: Spread each pizza crust with ½ cup seasoned tomato sauce, top with ½ cup marinated mussels and ¼ cup good quality lump crab meat. Sprinkle with minced garlic, grated Parmesan cheese and minced parsley.

Roadside

5

Tuna Noodle Casserole

TOM VALENTI

You will love this grown-up, sophisticated version of the American classic. For this recipe, Tom prefers pennette pasta, a smaller version of the penne, because it is about the same size as the tuna pieces and the center fills up with the creamy sauce, yielding a perfect balance of flavors and texture. Don't skimp on the quality of the tuna; it does make a big difference.

SIX SERVINGS

6 tablespoons butter

½ cup plus 2 tablespoons all-purpose flour

3 cups whole milk

1 large egg yolk

Salt and freshly ground black pepper to taste

¾ cup freshly grated Parmesan cheese

1 lb pennette pasta, cooked al dente and drained

One 12 oz can imported Italian or Spanish tuna packed in oil, drained

2 garlic cloves, peeled and minced

2 tablespoons minced oregano leaves or 1 tablespoon dried

2 tablespoons minced flat-leaf parsley

½ cup dried bread crumbs

Preheat the oven to 400° F.

Melt the butter in a heavy saucepan over medium heat. Add the flour and whisk until the mixture is smooth. Whisking constantly, add the milk a little at a time, making sure it is smooth and not lumpy before each addition. Turn off the heat.

Beat the egg yolk in a small mixing bowl; add 1 to 2 tablespoons flour and milk mixture and whisk until well combined. Pour the egg yolk mixture back into the pot. Stir in the Parmesan cheese and season with salt and pepper to taste.

Fold in the pasta, tuna, garlic, oregano and parsley and stir to blend the mixture and coat the pasta. Adjust seasoning with salt and pepper to taste. Pour into the gratin dish, shaking the pan to evenly distribute. Sprinkle with bread crumbs and bake 10 to 15 minutes until golden brown and crusty on top.

Recipe adapted from Soups, Stews and One-Pot Meals. Tom Valenti and Andrew Friedman (Scribner, 2003)

Fettuccine with Smoked Salmon and Dill

MINUTEMEALS CHEFS

Smoked salmon and smoked fish in general are very versatile travel companions. They have a long shelf life and can be turned on a whim into all sorts of culinary creations—from elegant canapés to more substantial main courses such as this pasta. When preparing this pasta or any other hot preparation, keep in mind that it is best to toss the smoked fish at the end of the cooking time. If the fish gets over-cooked, it will change taste and texture. Smoked trout would work equally well in this recipe.

FOUR SERVINGS

1 lb fettuccine
1 tablespoon vegetable oil
1 large shallot, minced
2 tablespoons capers (optional)
⅔ cup dry white wine
1 cup heavy cream

1 cup frozen peas, thawed
1 large tomato, chopped
⅓ cup chopped fresh dill or 1 tablespoon dried
12 oz smoked salmon, cut into ½-inch strips

Bring a large pot of lightly salted water to a boil over high heat. Add the pasta and cook according to the package directions, stirring occasionally until al dente. Drain.

Meanwhile, heat the vegetable oil in a large skillet over high heat. Add the minced shallot and cook, stirring for 1 minute. Add the capers (optional) and the white wine. Bring to a boil and reduce the wine for 5 minutes. Add the heavy cream and reduce the mixture for 3 minutes until the cream is slightly thickened.

Add the peas, chopped tomato, dill and the pasta. Gently toss to coat and simmer for 1 to 2 minutes until all the ingredients are hot. Stir in the smoked salmon and serve immediately.

Adapted from Minutemeals.com

Pasta Tuna Puttanesca

MINUTEMEALS CHEFS

From the kitchens of the chefs at Minutemeals, here is a satisfying pasta entree that can be assembled in a snap with ingredients found in the average cupboard. This dish is equally delicious served hot or at room temperature.

FOUR SERVINGS

1 lb spaghetti

2 tablespoons olive oil

3 anchovy fillets (or to taste), rinsed and chopped

3 garlic cloves, chopped

One 35 oz can whole Italian tomatoes, drained and coarsely chopped

Red pepper flakes to taste

2 tablespoons drained capers

One 6 oz can tuna in oil, drained and broken into small pieces

1 cup pitted Kalamata olives

2 tablespoons minced parsley, basil or fresh oregano, or any combination

Salt and freshly ground pepper to taste

Bring a large pot of lightly salted water to a boil. Add the pasta, stir to separate the strands and cook according to the directions on the package until al dente. Drain well in a colander.

Meanwhile, heat 2 tablespoons olive oil over medium heat in a large sauté pan. Add the garlic and anchovies and cook, stirring and pressing on the anchovies with a wooden spoon to form a paste. Add the tomatoes and red pepper flakes to taste, lower the heat and cook, stirring occasionally, for 5 to 7 minutes.

Stir in the capers and cook for 3 to 5 minutes. Add the tuna and olives to the sauce and stir well to blend. Simmer the sauce for 2 to 3 minutes. Adjust seasoning to taste with salt, pepper and red pepper flakes if desired.

Toss the pasta into the pan and stir to coat evenly with the sauce. Sprinkle with the fresh herbs and serve immediately.

Adapted from Minutemeals.com

Linguini with Creamy Basil Sauce

This pasta sauce is a pleasant alternative to the pesto. As a variation, toss skinny, crunchy steamed green beans with the pasta and sauce.

SIX SERVINGS

1 lb linguini pasta
2 garlic cloves, minced
½ cup ricotta cheese
¼ cup freshly grated Parmesan cheese
3 tablespoons olive oil

Salt and freshly ground pepper to taste
3 ripe tomatoes, seeded and diced
¾ cup chopped fresh basil leaves
¼ cup toasted pine nuts

Bring a large pot of lightly salted water to a boil over high heat. Add the pasta and cook according to the package directions, stirring occasionally until al dente. Drain.

Meanwhile, combine the garlic, ricotta, Parmesan cheese, olive oil, salt and pepper in a large serving bowl. Whisk until well blended.

Add the hot pasta to the bowl. Add the tomatoes, basil and pine nuts and toss to coat the pasta evenly. Adjust seasoning with salt and pepper and serve immediately.

Spring Vegetable Orzo "Risotto"

Here is a take on risotto primavera that doesn't require any stirring over a hot pot. Orzo is a rice-shaped pasta available in most supermarkets. Feel free to experiment with other vegetables of your choice as long as they are cut into small pieces.

FOUR SERVINGS

2 tablespoons olive oil
1 shallot, minced
1 ½ cups orzo pasta
4 cups chicken or vegetable broth
½ cup 1-inch pieces asparagus
¼ cup frozen peas

2 tablespoons minced Italian parsley
1 tablespoon minced fresh basil
  or mint
1 tablespoon butter (optional)
¼ cup freshly grated Parmesan
  cheese, plus additional for serving

Heat the olive oil in a heavy large saucepan over medium-low heat. Add the shallot and sauté until wilted and translucent, about 5 minutes. Do not brown.

Add the orzo and cook, stirring for 1 to 2 minutes until the orzo is well coated. Add the chicken broth and bring to a boil. Reduce the heat to medium-low, cover and cook for 6 to 8 minutes, stirring once in a while until the orzo begins to soften.

Add the asparagus; cover and cook for another 6 minutes until the asparagus is tender. Stir in the peas and cook uncovered until the liquid is almost gone. Remove from the heat and stir in the herbs, butter (optional) and grated cheese. Transfer to a serving bowl and serve immediately.

Wine Racks

Few of us road warriors have the luxury of Molly and Donn Chappellet, who as wine makers can stock their RV wine cellar with some favorite varietals and vintages from their Napa winery. But to some other RVers, we suggest you stash a bottle or two of your favorite vintage wine as well as a bottle of Champagne or sparkling wine for impromptu celebrations.

As for which wine with which dish, we advise you to keep it simple: all around casual wines can be enjoyed with fish or meat and everything in between.

For reds: a juicy Merlot, a refreshing Beaujolais or a fruity Chianti are always good choices. They are best drunk slightly chilled.

If your taste runs to white wines or rosés, a buttery Chardonnay, a zingy Chenin Blanc or zesty Sauvignon Blanc are always delicious and reliable choices, while a dry yet flavorful White Zinfandel or a French Rosé are sure-fire festive and refreshing alternatives.

Nowadays, a growing number of winemakers are starting to sell their everyday table wine varietals in convenient, recyclable, one-liter tetra pak containers. Brands such as **French Rabbit** offer easy drinking whites and reds in attractive packaging that is light, easy to store and eco-friendly.

Pop the cork or open the screw top and enjoy!

Asian Chicken Noodle Salad

PRISCILLA MARTEL

For an Asian flavor fix with little fuss, try this colorful salad of crisp vegetable slaw, crunchy noodles and chicken. Mundane fare packaged ramen noodle soup is its surprise ingredient. Ramen are pre-cooked and dried and can be eaten without further preparation right out of their packaging. Priscilla prefers serving this salad shortly after it is assembled while the noodles are still wild and crunchy. For a softer version, allow the mixture to sit for 3 to 4 hours before serving.

FOUR SERVINGS

FOR THE DRESSING:
1 ½ tablespoons rice wine vinegar
2 tablespoons fresh lime juice
2 teaspoons soy sauce
One 1-inch piece of peeled fresh
    ginger
½ teaspoon salt
3 tablespoons peanut oil
1 ½ tablespoons sesame oil
Freshly ground pepper to taste

FOR THE SALAD:
3 cups packaged broccoli slaw,
    available in most grocery stores
3 scallions, trimmed, finely chopped
2 packages ramen noodles
    (seasoning packets reserved)
2 boneless, skinless chicken breasts,
    about 6 oz each
2 teaspoons vegetable oil for grilling
1 lime quartered for garnish

Combine the rice wine vinegar, lime juice and soy sauce in a large salad bowl. Grate the ginger into the bowl using the fine side of a grater. Add the salt and whisk in the peanut and sesame oils.

Add the broccoli slaw and scallions to the dressing. Break the uncooked ramen noodles into the bowl, crushing them gently between your fingers until they are in nugget-sized pieces. Toss the salad to coat all the ingredients, then adjust the seasonings with salt and pepper to taste. Set aside.

Place the chicken breasts on a cutting board. Using a meat mallet or the bottom of a flat skillet, lightly pound the breasts to flatten them to a uniform thickness of about ½-inch. Sprinkle the chicken with some of the reserved ramen seasoning, your favorite Asian-style rub or salt and pepper. Coat the meat with the vegetable oil.

Just before serving, grill the chicken over medium-high heat on a grill pan or outdoor grill for about 3 to 4 minutes until lightly marked on 1 side. Flip each piece of chicken and cook on the other side for another 3 to 4 minutes, or until cooked through.

To serve, divide the slaw between 4 plates. Cut the chicken into long strips ½-inch wide. Place some of the chicken on each plate. Garnish with wedges of fresh lime.

TIP *Pressed for time? Prepare this salad with a store-bought roast chicken and a good quality ginger and sesame dressing. Leftover grilled chicken will also do.*

Priscilla Martel

When it comes to the culinary biz, Priscilla seems to have done it all. A former chef and restaurateur, she is now a consultant, a teacher and food writer with a special interest in artisan baking, the pastry arts and the foods of the Mediterranean. But to her friends, she is one of the most gracious accomplished hostesses around. Few pass up the opportunity to attend one her many gatherings, whether it's a cook-out, a picnic or a simple meal by the fire in her Connecticut home.

Over the years, as a home cook, Priscilla has developed some fantastic recipes that are always delicious, festive and effortless. Her contributing recipes to *Cooking on the Road with Celebrity Chefs* are tasty travel companions, but you will want to keep them handy once you get home.

Book Stash

The Best Bread Ever: Great Home Made Bread Using Your Food Processor
by Charles Van Over and Priscilla Martel (Broadway Books, 1997)

On Baking: A Textbook of Baking and Culinary Fundamentals
by Priscilla Martel, Sarah Labensky, Eddy van Damme and Klaus Tenbergen
(Prentice Hall, 2004)

On Cooking: A Textbook of Culinary Fundamentals, 4th Edition
by Priscilla Martel, Sarah Labensky, Alan M. Hause and Steve Labensky
(Prentice Hall, 2006)

Tooling Around

Whether a professional chef or a home cook, everyone has a favorite kitchen tool. Spatulas and wooden spoons, a whisk, 1or 2 sturdy tongs and a pair of mixing bowls should be enough to get you by. In addition, here are a few things you'll always find in our chefs' tool box.

Craig Shelton won't leave his home kitchen without silicone oven mitts. They are heat-resistant up to 500° F; you can retrieve a lobster in boiling water or grab a dish out of the oven without burning yourself. Invest in the most flexible pair with a good grip to prevent slipping. These colorful mitts are available in good cookware stores or online.

Cooking on a grill or an open fire is part of the fun, but it can be hard on any cookware. Instead of lugging heavy cast-iron pans, *Charlie Palmer* packs a couple of inexpensive, lightweight aluminum nonstick pans that can be discarded after extensive wear and tear.

A low-tech guy, *Daniel Bruce* packs Dr. Bronner's Liquid Soap (WWW.DRBRONNER.COM) and uses it for practically everything from shampooing to laundry and washing dishes. The organic soap comes in many scents—peppermint is the Bruce's family favorite. A neat trick he learned over the years to minimize pot scrubbing: Daniel rubs the outside bottom of the pot with a drop or two of liquid soap before using. The grime will slip off easily during washing.

Among *Jamie Roraback's* grilling paraphernalia, you'll find his trusty meat thermometer, which he inserts in practically everything that hits the grill. His guidelines are as follows: 145° F for fish and pork, 155° F for ground beef and ground pork and 165° F for chicken and turkey.

Ramen Noodle Soup with Shrimp and Spinach

ZAK PELACCIO

Everybody loves ramen noodles! In this recipe, Zak gives them his own spin by seasoning the broth at first, lending the soup its distinct flavors. Once this is done, the combination of ingredients is endless—tofu, smoked meat, broccoli, carrots etc. Let your imagination guide you. It is also an excellent way to recycle leftovers such as grilled or roasted poultry or beef. Cut up or shred the meat and add at the end just to warm up. Don't forget to pack your chopsticks.

FOUR TO SIX SERVINGS

2 tablespoons vegetable oil
2 celery stalks, thinly sliced
1 medium onion, thinly sliced
One 3-inch piece ginger, peeled and thinly sliced
4 garlic cloves, thinly sliced
10 cups low-sodium chicken broth
1 cup frozen peas
24 frozen shrimp, thawed and peeled
4 packages ramen noodles (discard seasoning packets)

One 10 oz package frozen spinach, thawed and excess water squeezed out
1 jalapeño pepper, seeded and thinly sliced
3 tablespoons soy sauce or more to taste
1 tablespoon sesame oil

Heat the vegetable oil in a large saucepan over medium heat. Add the celery, onion, garlic and ginger slices and cook until softened and translucent, making sure not to brown, about 5 minutes. Add the chicken broth and bring to a boil. Reduce to a simmer and cook for 30 minutes. Strain the flavored broth into a clean saucepan. The broth can be prepared ahead and refrigerated for 2 days or frozen for up to 1 month.

When ready to serve, bring the broth back to a boil. Add the peas and cook for 1 minute. Add the shrimp and cook for 1 minute; add the noodles and cook for 2 minutes. Add the spinach, soy sauce and jalapeño and simmer for another minute. Ladle the soup into 4 serving bowls and drizzle each serving with the sesame oil.

Chef
Zak Pelaccio

EXECUTIVE CHEF
5 Ninth Restaurant, New York City
Fatty Crab, New York City

Trailing Zak

Depending on the time of day, he may be at his upscale restaurant, 5 Ninth, located in the trendy Meatpacking district of Manhattan, or just a few blocks away at his tiny hole-in-a-wall Malaysian eatery. Just a few years ago, the talented, young chef entered the New York dining scene with a bang. He quickly won over culinary critics with his interpretation of New York's global cuisine along with his personal rendition of Asian food.

Unknown Trails

After graduating from the French Culinary Institute, Zak pondered becoming a chef (he was also contemplating going to medical school), and took some time off to backpack through Southeast Asia. Traveling from town to town, meeting with home cooks and local chefs, the gourmet globe-trotter developed an intimate knowledge of the native ingredients of the region, its spices and their numerous uses. Overall, this on-the-go education was very revealing and fruitful. And for the pleasure of his future patrons, upon his return, Zak took up cooking in earnest.

Happy Trails

Well they were not camping exactly, as it happened in the dead of winter in snowy Vermont. But a few years ago, the very romantic Zak convinced his girlfriend, Ana, to follow him on a midnight hike up a frozen mountain trail. The ring, champagne flutes and bubbly were safely hidden in his bag.

Mom and Dad's Trails

While growing up, camping and trekking out West was a favorite vacation of the Pelaccios, parents and children alike. Every year brought a new adventure: The Grand Teton in Wyoming one year, Glacier National Park in Montana the next, etc. They all had grand times, and according to all reports, Zak's mom became quite an expert at doctoring up instant soups and mashed potatoes, as well as dried beef jerky. The only sour note for the young Pelaccios was wearing bells tied to their shoes to scare off bears for the entire trip (Mom's idea), and definitely not cool when you're ten!

Dream Trails

Like his parents before him, Zak would love to take his son, Hudson, to explore the back roads of this country and its amazing landscapes. But this time, no bells on shoes and no dehydrated food. He's thinking RV all the way!

Fatty Crab

643 Hudson Street
New York, NY 10014
212-352-3590
WWW.FATTYCRAB.COM

5 Ninth Restaurant

5 Ninth Avenue
New York, NY 10014
212-929-9460
WWW.5NINTH.COM

Polenta with Mushroom and Tomato Ragout

ZAK PELACCIO

Stash a couple of packets of dried mushrooms in your RV pantry—a quick soak in hot water and minimal chopping and they are ready for action. They add wonderful earthy flavors to soups, stews and quick sauces to be spooned over grilled cuts of meat or tossed over pasta. Or try them in this rustic, assertive entree served over creamy polenta.

FOUR SERVINGS

2 oz dried mushrooms such as porcini, chanterelles, shitake or oyster, or any combination
¼ cup olive oil
2 garlic cloves, minced
1 medium onion, minced
2 stalks celery, minced
4 thick slices bacon, cut into ½-inch pieces (optional)

2 tablespoons tomato paste
One 14 oz can whole tomatoes
Pinch dried red pepper flakes to taste
1 cup instant polenta
Salt to taste
¼ cup grated Parmesan Reggiano
2 tablespoons minced parsley leaves

Place the mushrooms in a bowl, cover with boiling water and soak for 30 minutes. Drain and rinse the mushrooms to remove any grits. Squeeze out any excess liquid. Coarsely chop the mushrooms and set aside.

Heat 1 tablespoon olive oil in a large saucepan over medium-high heat. Add the onion, garlic, celery and bacon (optional) and cook without browning until the vegetables are soft and translucent. Add the mushrooms and cook, stirring once in a while, for 5 minutes over medium heat. Stir in the tomato paste and cook for 2 minutes.

Add the canned tomatoes and their juice to the pan and bring to a simmer. Season with the dried pepper flakes and salt to taste and lightly crush the tomatoes with the back of a spoon. Cover the pan and simmer for 30 minutes. Prepare the polenta according to the package instructions. Fold in the remaining olive oil and the Parmesan cheese at the end of the cooking. The polenta should be creamy, not stiff.

Divide the polenta among 6 serving plates. Make a well at the center of each serving and ladle the ragout over it. Garnish with the chopped parsley.

Herb Rice with Toasted Nuts

This appetizing vibrant rice is terrific served with meat and poultry, either grilled or braised. Adjust the amount of herbs according to your taste or experiment with other flavors such as mint or chives.

SIX SERVINGS

2 teaspoons olive oil
2 ½ cups long-grain white rice
1 ½ cups loosely packed cilantro
  leaves
½ cup loosely packed basil leaves

½ cup toasted nuts such as walnuts,
  hazelnuts, pine nuts or any
  combination, coarsely chopped
Salt and freshly ground pepper to
  taste

Bring 4 ½ quarts water to a boil.

Heat the oil in a large heavy saucepan over medium-high heat. Add the rice and sauté for 3 minutes until well coated. Pour in the boiling water, season with salt, stir and cover tightly. Lower the heat to simmer and cook for 20 minutes. Turn off the heat and let stand covered for 5 minutes.

Mince the herbs and stir into the rice along with the toasted nuts. Adjust seasonings with salt and pepper and serve immediately.

Curried Basmati Rice

CYNTHIA KELLER

This is a comforting dish Cynthia usually prepares after a day of hiking or fishing. She serves this savory rice with her Grilled Lemongrass Chicken on page 80.

SIX SERVINGS

2 tablespoons butter
1 small onion, finely minced
1 tablespoon curry powder
1 small cinnamon stick
1 bay leaf

1 pinch saffron threads
2 cups basmati rice
½ teaspoon kosher salt
½ cup golden raisins
¼ cup chopped peanuts

Bring 2 ¼ cups water to a boil.

In a saucepan with tight fitting lid, melt the butter over medium heat. Add the onion and sauté until translucent, 4 to 5 minutes. Add the curry powder, cinnamon stick, bay leaf and saffron. Cook, stirring constantly, for 1 to 2 minutes.

Add the rice and sauté for 1 minute, stirring to coat the grains evenly with the spices and butter. Add the boiling water and salt, and bring back to a boil. Reduce the heat to a very low simmer, cover the pot and continue cooking for 10 minutes.

Remove from the heat and let the rice rest, covered, for at least 5 minutes or until ready to serve. Just before serving, add the raisins and peanuts and fluff the rice with a fork.

TIP   Measure out the rice and pack it in an airtight container along with the dried spices.

One-Pot Red Beans, Rice and Sausage

JIMMY BANNOS

These red beans can be cooked on a grill, gas burner, even a campfire. If cooking on an open fire, do not use a pot with plastic handles, which will burn or melt; keep in mind that the intensity of the heat source will vary the cooking time. In any case, the result is an inviting blend of flavors and textures. Serve it as a side dish or right out of the pot as a main course for two.

FOUR SERVINGS

1 teaspoon olive oil
4 oz smoked sausage, preferably andouille, cut into ½-inch dice
1 small yellow onion, finely chopped
½ green bell pepper (or any color), seeded and chopped
1 garlic clove, minced
½ teaspoon Creole seasoning

Pinch of red pepper flakes
½ cup converted white rice
1 ½ cups hot water
One 15 ½ oz can light red kidney beans, drained
Hot sauce (optional)
Salt (optional)

If using a grill, preheat to high.

Add the oil to a medium size pot and heat until hot. Add the sausage and sauté until lightly browned. Stir in the onion, bell pepper, garlic, Creole seasoning and red pepper flakes. Cook, stirring occasionally for 4 to 5 minutes until vegetables are soft. If cooking on a grill, close the grill top to increase the charcoal or gas temperature if necessary.

Stir in the rice, water and beans. Bring to a simmer, cover with a tight fitting lid or heavy duty aluminum foil and cook 15 minutes. Make sure that the mixture is simmering, not boiling. Carefully remove the lid (the steam can be very hot), stir the mixture, cover the pot and cook an additional 5 to 7 minutes.

Remove the pot from the grill and let it rest, covered, for 5 to 10 minutes. Test to ensure rice is cooked through. If desired, season with the hot sauce and salt to taste. Serve immediately.

Chef
Jimmy Bannos

CHEF/OWNER
Heaven on Seven Restaurants in Chicago

Nola on Lake Michigan

You won't find a chef more passionate about New Orleans than Jimmy Bannos. Twenty years ago, the Chicago-based third generation restaurateur and chef brought dozens of Crescent City culinary classics north to the Windy City. Fresh out of cooking school, the budding chef was fascinated by the Big Easy's multifaceted culture, its vast and diverse food heritage and spicy heat. After multiple extended trips, young Jimmy convinced his parents to transform the family coffee shop into Heaven on Seven, which became an overnight success. Enthusiasts and aficionados flocked to the place for his thick gumbos, flavorful jambalayas and heady Creole and Cajun creations. Today, you can also catch Jimmy and his exciting cuisine on the "Today Show" on NBC where he is a frequent contributor.

Spicing Things Up

Heaven on Seven restaurants are fun and congenial, and give out enough heat to melt the ice on Lake Michigan in the dead of winter. Besides this superlative cuisine there is plenty of quirkiness to go around and keep diners interested. One of them is Jimmy's "Wall of Fire," an extensive and impressive collection of hot sauces from around the world. What started as a fun, spontaneous idea is now part of the Heaven on Seven culture. Patrons are encouraged to contribute unique hot sauces gathered around the world to add to the expanding shrine.

Camp Cooking

OK, one wouldn't call Jimmy an RV enthusiast trailing along open roads, and never mind tent camping! However, Jimmy travels a lot for his many charity events, book tours and consulting. On his down time, he likes to stay close to home. But a few years ago, he became a familiar face at some of the RV parks around the country. Just as he did 20 years ago when he introduced great New Orleans grub to the Windy City, with great enthusiasm and showmanship, Jimmy is opening new culinary frontiers to RVers and campers. His cooking demonstrations are always fun, insightful and rewarding, and whether he is teaching the art of spicing things up or expert grilling, they are always delicious.

Book Stash

The Heaven on Seven Cookbook
by Jimmy Bannos and John Demers (Ten Speed Press, 2001)

Big Easy Cocktails
by Jimmy Bannos and John Demers (Ten Speed Press, 2005)

To make a contribution to the "Wall of Fire" or simply have a great meal:

Heaven on Seven on Wabash
111 N. Wabash Avenue
Chicago, Il 60602.
312-263-6443

Heaven on Seven on Rush
600 N. Michigan Avenue.
2nd floor. Chicago, Il 60611
312-280-7774

Heaven on Seven in Naperville
224 South Main St
Naperville, Il 60540
630-717-0777

WWW.HEAVENONSEVEN.COM

Cool Salads

AND SAVORY SIDE DISHES

Warm Couscous Salad

CHARLIE PALMER

Quick-cooking couscous is a terrific starch to keep on hand as it takes minimal preparation and combines beautifully with vegetables or fruits to make a very tasty side dish. This salad can be made in a pot over an open fire or on a hot grill as well as on the stove top in an RV kitchen. It is delicious served warm, but it also tastes great at room temperature or chilled.

FOUR SERVINGS

¼ cup golden raisins or dried currants

1 ¼ cups quick cooking couscous

Chicken broth (optional)

¼ cup minced red onion

2 tablespoons chopped fresh flat-leaf parsley

1 tablespoon chopped fresh mint leaves or any fresh herbs available

2 tablespoons pine nuts, chopped almonds or pecans (optional)

1 teaspoon freshly grated orange zest (optional)

¼ cup olive oil

Juice of 1 lemon or to taste

Coarse salt and freshly ground pepper to taste

Place the raisins (or currants) in hot water to cover and set aside to plump for about 15 minutes. When plump, drain well and set aside.

Cook the couscous according to the package directions using either water or chicken broth.

When all of the liquid has been absorbed, add the raisins, onion, parsley and mint and, if using, the orange zest and nuts. Add the olive oil and lemon juice and using a dinner fork, toss to fluff the grains and incorporate the other ingredients. Adjust seasoning with salt and pepper to taste and serve hot or at room temperature.

Shrimp and Avocado Salad

PRISCILLA MARTEL

At her guests' request, this salad is a staple at Priscilla's parties. It tastes delicious and looks very festive. While store-bought cooked shrimp can be used, the extra step of cooking them yourself will make this simple salad even better.

FOUR SERVINGS

½ lb unpeeled raw shrimp or 5 oz peeled and cooked shrimp
¼ cup prepared mayonnaise
2 teaspoons ketchup
1 teaspoon Cognac or brandy
1 tablespoon chopped fresh parsley

Salt and freshly ground pepper to taste
2 ripe Haas avocados
Chopped parsley and salad greens for garnish (optional)

Add the shrimp to 1 quart of salted boiling water. Bring the water back to a boil over high heat and cook for 1 more minute. Drain the shrimp. Let them cool, then peel them.

While the shrimp cool, prepare the dressing. Combine the mayonnaise, ketchup and Cognac in a small bowl. Stir until the mixture is evenly pink in color. Season with salt and black pepper to taste. Stir in the peeled shrimp and the chopped parsley.

Split each avocado in ½ laterally from top to bottom. Remove each pit, place 2 halves on serving plates and top with the shrimp salad. Garnish with more chopped parsley and some colorful greens, if desired.

Fresh Mozzarella and Watermelon Salad with Purple Basil

CHEF HARRY

This salad is a refreshing crunchy variation on the classic Italian tomato and mozzarella combo. Serve it with sliced French bread brushed with olive oil, lightly toasted or grilled.

SIX TO EIGHT SERVINGS

2 cups seeded small watermelon balls

2 cups diced fresh mozzarella

1 cup chopped fresh purple basil

1 bunch scallions, trimmed and chopped

⅓ cup olive oil

Salt and freshly ground pepper to taste

3 cups loosely packed baby greens

Balsamic vinegar to taste

Toss together the watermelon, mozzarella, basil, scallions and oil in a mixing bowl. Season with salt and pepper to taste.

Spread the greens on a serving platter and spoon the watermelon salad over them. If desired, drizzle with balsamic vinegar and serve.

TIP Purple basil is milder than its green counterpart and adds a lovely vibrancy to this colorful salad. Look for it at farmers' markets and organic grocers. If you fail in your quest, you may substitute fresh green basil.

Panzanella Salad

PATRICIA WILLIAMS

The secret to this simple but flavorful Tuscan salad is using vegetables at their peak—seek out a farmer's stand before pulling up for the night and you will be well rewarded. Traditionally prepared with moistened day-old bread, this version has a nice crunch from the crisp croutons thrown in just before serving.

FOUR SERVINGS

½ quart mixed cherry tomatoes, halved
¼ cup diced red pepper
¼ cup diced yellow pepper
½ cup diced chayote or yellow squash
2 cups roasted corn kernels

1 ½ cups fresh basil, cut into thin strips
½ cup lime juice
1 ½ cups croutons, toasted
Coarse salt to taste
Freshly ground pepper to taste
½ cup olive oil

Combine the tomatoes, red and yellow peppers, chayote or squash and the roasted corn in a serving bowl. Set aside in a cool place until ready to serve.

Just before serving, toss in the croutons, basil, lime juice and olive oil. Adjust seasonings with salt and pepper to taste.

Tangy Vegetable Slaw

JACK HIGGINS

This lemony crunchy slaw is an outstanding companion to any grilled meat and sandwiches such as Zak's Sloppy Joes (page 25). Jack recommends serving his slaw folded into his "Barbecue" Pulled Pork Sandwich (page 34).

EIGHT TO TEN SERVINGS

1 ¼ lbs cabbage, finely shredded
¾ lb carrots, finely shredded
1 green pepper, thinly sliced
1 red pepper, thinly sliced
1 medium onion, thinly sliced
1 ½ cups mayonnaise

¼ cup plus 2 tablespoons cider vinegar
Juice of 1 lemon
½ teaspoon celery seeds
1 tablespoon sugar
Salt and freshly ground pepper to taste

Layer the cabbage, carrots, peppers and onion in a large serving bowl.

Combine the mayonnaise, vinegar, lemon juice, celery seeds, sugar and salt and pepper in a small mixing bowl. Whisk the mixture until smooth and creamy and the sugar is dissolved.

Pour the dressing over the vegetables and toss well to combine. Adjust seasonings with salt, pepper and lemon juice to taste. Cover and refrigerate for 1 hour before serving to allow the flavors to blend.

Orange and Avocado Salad
MINUTEMEALS CHEFS

Here is an unusual take on the classic Mediterranean fennel and orange combo. By all means, if you find yourself with a stray fennel bulb, substitute it for the avocado. And if you have neither on hand, simply slice the oranges, dot with pitted olives and add a pinch of ground cumin and a few parsley leaves to the dressing for an outstanding Moroccan-inspired salad.

FOUR SERVINGS

1 navel orange
1 firm and ripe avocado
⅓ cup pitted marinated olives
1 tablespoon olive oil
1 tablespoon red wine vinegar

Salt and freshly ground pepper to taste
3 cups pre-washed mixed salad greens

With a sharp knife, remove the peel and white membrane from the orange. Quarter the orange lengthwise and slice. Pit, peel and dice the avocado. Coarsely chop the olives.

In a salad bowl, combine the orange slices, avocado, olives, oil, vinegar, salt and pepper. Top with the salad greens and toss. Serve immediately.

Adapted from Minutemeals.com

Cobb Salad

CRAIG SHELTON

This American classic earned Craig his Merit Badge in cooking. Many years later, it is still a winner. For best results, toss with the dressing just before serving.

FOUR SERVINGS

6 strips bacon
¾ cup vegetable oil
½ cup cider vinegar
2 tablespoons lemon juice
2 teaspoons Dijon mustard
2 tablespoons minced parsley
Salt and freshly ground pepper to taste
1 large head romaine lettuce

2 ripe tomatoes, seeded and cut into wedges
1 avocado, peeled and cut into thin wedges
2 celery stalks, thinly sliced
4 scallions, thinly sliced
¾ lb turkey breast, cubed
½ cup crumbled blue cheese

Cook the bacon in a small skillet until crisp and golden brown. Remove from the pan and drain on paper towels.

In a mixing bowl, whisk together the oil, vinegar, lemon juice, mustard, parsley, salt and pepper.

Tear the lettuce leaves into bite size pieces and place them in a salad bowl. Toss with half of the vinaigrette. Layer the tomatoes, avocado, celery, scallions and turkey on top of the romaine. Drizzle the remaining vinaigrette and garnish with the crumbled blue cheese and bacon. Serve immediately.

Green Markets

Chefs are great advocates and a driving force behind sustainable agriculture, utilizing produce from local farms as often as possible. While traveling through this country's wilderness, buying local may not be an option, but a little investigating before leaving home may be useful. There are a few online resources worth checking out. Many cities' and communities' websites list the location, time and days of operation for their local farmers' markets. On the Local Harvest website WWW.LOCALHARVEST.ORG you'll find, among other things, an interactive nationwide directory for local farms, markets and products. And if you drive by a farm stand, by all means make sure to stop.

Roasted Leek and Potato Salad

GUY MICHAUD

This fresh and lemony potato salad is at its best served warm or at room temperature. It will complement any grilled meat or fish and, for a change of pace, make an interesting starch to a saucy stew in lieu of mashed potatoes or pasta. Traveling in early spring? Be sure to look for a farmer's stand offering freshly harvested ramps (wild leeks), and use 8 to 10 bulbs instead of regular leeks:

FOUR SERVINGS

4 small young leeks, white part only, trimmed and washed, or 8 to 10 ramps
1 tablespoon olive oil
Salt and freshly ground pepper to taste
1 lb new potatoes

¾ cup mayonnaise
1 heaping tablespoon minced chives
2 tablespoons minced parsley
1 shallot, minced
Juice of ½ lemon or more to taste
1 to 2 tablespoons Champagne or red wine vinegar

Note: The leeks can also be roasted on a grill for 4 to 5 minutes on each side.

Preheat the oven to 375° F.

Halve the leeks lengthwise and place on a baking sheet. Add the olive oil, salt and pepper and toss to coat. Roast in the oven for about 20 minutes (10 minutes if using ramps) until soft and lightly charred. Remove from the oven and cool.

Cook the potatoes in simmering salted water until tender, about 15 minutes. Drain and set aside.

Meanwhile, in a large serving bowl, combine the mayonnaise, chives, parsley and shallot. Whisk in lemon juice and vinegar until smooth and creamy. Adjust seasoning to taste with salt and freshly ground pepper and additional lemon juice or vinegar.

When the potatoes are cool enough to handle, quarter and toss them into the dressing. Chop the leeks coarsely and add to the potatoes. Toss well to combine and set aside for 30 minutes at room temperature before serving, allowing the flavors to blend.

German Potato Salad

GUY MICHAUD

Guy learned this recipe from one of his first cooking instructors. To his mind and to his friends and family, it is still the ultimate potato salad.

FOUR SERVINGS

1 lb small red new potatoes

4 thick slices applewood-smoked
   bacon, cut into ¼-inch pieces

1 onion, thinly sliced

1 teaspoon fresh thyme

2 to 3 tablespoons Dijon mustard

2 tablespoons olive oil

Salt and freshly ground black
   pepper to taste

1 tablespoon wine vinegar (optional)

Cook the potatoes in lightly salted water until soft but still firm, about 15 minutes. Drain and cool.

In a skillet, cook the bacon over medium-low heat until crisp and golden brown. Remove with a slotted spoon and drain on paper towels. Discard half the fat from the pan. Add the onion slices and thyme to the skillet and cook over medium-high heat until the onion is wilted and lightly browned, about 5 minutes.

Pour the onion mixture into a serving bowl. Add the mustard, olive oil, salt and pepper and whisk together to combine. Quarter the potatoes and crumble the bacon. Add them to the bowl and toss until well combined. Adjust seasoning to taste. The dressing should have enough acidity from the mustard. If it is not enough to your taste, add 1 tablespoon wine vinegar.

Chef
Guy Michaud

Campanile in Los Angeles

Trailing Guy

A chef-in-training working in some of the country's best kitchens, Guy is currently a line cook at Mark Peel's star-studded Campanile in Los Angeles. After graduating from cooking school, Guy embarked on his culinary journey in New York's East Village, a breeding ground for cutting-edge cuisine and new talents. After learning all he could from these innovative chefs, Guy moved out West to explore the California way around the kitchen.

Exploring New Paths

Guy didn't set out to become a chef; the revelation came in a round-about way. He grew up in London and moved to the States as a teenage guitarist in a rock band, looking to make a career of it—a dream he pursued for six years. Between gigs, he held a series of jobs in assorted fields; the one that stuck was cooking.

European Open Roads

From London, the Michaud family took many summer vacations to Portugal and Spain, traveling in a Volvo with two tents and staying at many campgrounds along the way. He remembers those trips fondly. His dad prepared the hearty English breakfasts on a campfire and they often dined at small local restaurants, where young Guy gorged on Portuguese spicy fish stew. Less happy memories remain of his school's camping trips to Northern England. The weather was cold and damp and the daily fare was a not so exotic canned beans and toast.

Open Roads USA

Guy has already traveled the back roads of New England. But he and his wife, Sarah, would love to explore the Grand Canyon someday—from the vantage point of an old-fashioned Airstream trailer.

Campanile

624 South La Brea Avenue
Los Angeles, CA 90036
323-938-1447

End of Summer Tomato and Avocado Salad

MOLLY CHAPPELLET

This salad is about tomatoes and avocados at their best. Molly serves it with a platter of steamed string beans and crusty French bread to round out her satisfying vegetarian meal. Ideally, the tomatoes should come from a local farmer's market or stand. The avocado should be ripe but still firm, serving as a contrasting texture to the tomatoes. Serve with chilled Chappellet Chardonnay.

TWO TO THREE SERVINGS

3 very ripe tomatoes, preferably from a farmer's market
1 ripe but firm avocado
Sea salt and freshly ground black pepper to taste
½ cup crumbled mild Feta cheese (preferably French)
2 to 3 tablespoons chopped basil to taste

½ cup pitted Kalamata olives, halved
1 to 2 tablespoons roasted hazelnuts, coarsely chopped
1 to 2 tablespoons pumpkin seeds or sunflower seeds
½ cup olive oil
2 tablespoons red wine vinegar
1 tablespoon honey mustard

Peel and cut the tomatoes into large chunks. Place in a bowl.

Peel the avocado and cut in similar size chunks. Add them to the bowl and drizzle with 1 to 2 tablespoons olive oil. Season with fresh pepper and sea salt and toss to combine.

Spread the salad in a serving platter and top with the Feta, basil, Kalamata olives, roasted hazelnuts and pumpkin or sunflower seed.

In a small mixing bowl, whisk together the remaining olive oil with the vinegar and honey mustard. Pour the dressing over the salad and toss lightly to combine. Adjust seasoning to taste with salt and pepper and serve immediately.

Apple and Asian Pear Fall Salad

MOLLY CHAPPELLET

Follow this recipe as a guideline; it is really a freeform salad that takes on a different personality depending on what dried fruits and nuts are hidden in your cupboard. Molly prefers Meyer lemons for the dressing, which are sweeter and less acidic than the common variety. If not available, use a regular lemon and adjust the amount to taste. Donn and Molly enjoy it with a glass of their own Chenin Blanc.

FOUR SERVINGS

2 crisp apples such as Cortland, McIntosh or Granny Smith
1 Asian pear
Juice of 1 Meyer lemon
4 to 5 tender celery ribs
½ cup mayonnaise
2 tablespoons sour cream
2 tablespoons chopped dried cranberries, currants or dates, or more to taste

2 tablespoons chopped toasted pecans, filberts or pumpkin seeds, or more to taste
Few fresh grapes (optional)
Salt and freshly ground pepper to taste

Peel and core the apples and pear and rub with the lemon juice.

Chop the celery, apples and pears and place in a serving bowl.

Whisk together the mayonnaise and sour cream until smooth and well blended. Fold into the salad. Adjust seasoning to taste with salt, pepper and lemon juice. Sprinkle with the dried fruit, nuts and grapes (optional) and serve immediately.

Grilled Corn with Herb Butter

LAURENT TOURONDEL

Grilling fresh corn in the husk keeps the kernels tender and moist. In this recipe the corn is infused with bright herb flavors while roasting. If you have any butter left over, spread on grilled steaks or chicken breasts. As the butter melts and mingles with the meat juices, you'll have an instant silky sauce. For more ideas on flavored butter, check out page 197.

SIX SERVINGS

6 ears fresh corn, husks on
12 tablespoons unsalted butter, softened
3 tablespoons finely chopped parsley

1 shallot, finely chopped
2 tablespoons minced chives
1 garlic clove, finely chopped
Salt and freshly ground pepper to taste

Preheat the grill to high.

Pull down the corn husks, leaving them attached at the base. Remove and discard the silk and set aside.

In a mixing bowl, combine the butter with the parsley, shallot, chives and garlic. Blend with a fork until the mixture is smooth and well combined. At this point, the butter mixture can be rolled into a log, wrapped in plastic wrap and refrigerated or frozen until ready to use.

Spread 2 tablespoons of the mixture over each ear of corn and generously season with salt and pepper. Rewrap the husk around the corn and tie the ends with butcher's twine.

Grill the corn for 6 minutes, turning once. Cover the grill and cook for another 5 minutes. Serve immediately.

Note: This recipe can also be done on a stove-top grill pan. Preheat the pan until very hot, add the corn and cover tightly with aluminum foil. Cook for 3 minutes; give each ear ¼ turn. Repeat every 3 minutes until the corn is cooked on all sides for a total of 12 minutes.

Corn and Potato "Risotto"

NEAL FRASER

Whether the texture of your mashed potatoes of choice is smooth or lumpy, Neal's "risotto" should please both camps. The potatoes are gently poached in cream and chicken broth to a rich creamy puree strewn with small bites of the spud. The sweet corn and sharp goat cheese add layers of contrasting flavors. It is a superb complement to roast chicken, stews, grilled meats or Craig Shelton's Chicken Cordon Bleu on page 57.

FOUR SERVINGS

4 ears of corn, shucked

3 medium Yukon gold potatoes, peeled and cut into ½-inch dice

½ cup heavy cream

1 cup chicken broth

2 tablespoons fresh soft goat cheese, room temperature

Coarse salt and freshly ground black pepper to taste

¼ cup loosely packed chopped chives, or to taste

Remove the corn from the cob, scraping along the sides to extract the milky liquid. Stir it into the corn kernels.

Combine the corn, potatoes, cream and chicken broth in a heavy saucepan. Bring to a boil over high heat and cook for 2 minutes. Season with salt, lower the heat to medium-low and simmer, stirring once in a while until the potatoes are cooked and the mixture is creamy and the potatoes lumpy.

Remove the pan from the heat and beat in the goat cheese and chives. Adjust seasonings with salt and pepper and serve immediately.

Barbecued Sweet Corn on the Cob

DANIEL BRUCE

This tasty sauce will add new layers of flavor to your next platter of fresh corn on the cob! The no-fuss barbecue sauce can also be used as a superb basting glaze on grilled chicken or pork cutlets.

EIGHT SERVINGS

½ cup tomato puree
2 tablespoons molasses
1 teaspoon kosher salt
¼ teaspoon ground white pepper
3 tablespoons soy sauce
1 teaspoon chopped garlic

2 tablespoons balsamic vinegar
3 tablespoons olive oil
1 teaspoon finely chopped fresh oregano
8 ears fresh corn

Preheat the grill to medium-high.

Place the tomato puree, molasses, salt, white pepper, soy sauce, garlic, balsamic vinegar, olive oil and oregano in a mixing bowl. Whisk together until well blended.

Shuck the corn and generously brush the sauce over each ear. Place the corn on the grill and mark all sides, turning until cooked, about 3 minutes per side. Remove from the grill and brush with additional barbecue sauce. Serve immediately.

Savory Potatoes on the Grill

CHARLIE PALMER

Although Charlie cooks these savory potatoes on the grill, they could easily be prepared in a 400° F oven or even sautéed on top of the stove.

FOUR SERVINGS

1 lb very small creamer potatoes, washed and sliced crosswise
1 large sweet onion such as Vidalia or Maui, cut lengthwise into thin slices

1 teaspoon fresh rosemary
3 tablespoons olive oil
Sea salt and freshly ground pepper to taste

Preheat the grill to low.

Form a double layer of heavy duty foil into a square large enough to enfold the potatoes in a single layer.

Place the potatoes, onions and rosemary in a mixing bowl. Drizzle with the olive oil and season with salt and pepper to taste. Toss well to combine. Transfer the mixture to the center of the foil, spreading it out to a single layer. Pull up the sides and fold them into one another to tightly seal the packet.

Place the packet on the preheated grill and cook, turning frequently, for about 40 minutes or until the potatoes are cooked through. Unwrap and serve.

What-a-Tater

FRANK OTTOMANELLI

Serve these delicious potatoes with grilled or roasted sausages.

SIX SERVINGS

6 medium potatoes, skin on
Chef's salt to taste (see tip on
    page 99)
2 small green peppers, seeded and
    cut into thin strips

1 small onion, thinly sliced
6 tablespoons butter or olive oil
Aluminum foil

Preheat the oven to 350° F.

Scrub the potatoes and dry. Cut the potatoes into quarters and set aside.

Cut the aluminum foil into six 12 x 12 squares. Place one quartered potato at the center of one of the aluminum squares. Sprinkle with chef's salt and layer some pepper strips and onion slices on top. Add 1 tablespoon butter or olive oil to the vegetables. Pull up the sides of the foil and fold them into one another to tightly seal the packet. Repeat with the remaining ingredients.

Place the packets on a baking sheet and cook for about 30 minutes or until the potatoes are cooked through. Carefully open the packages and serve.

Quick Ratatouille

A true ratatouille is time consuming and very involved. This version is a lot simpler and faster without compromising its complex flavors. Leftovers are delicious cold tossed with a touch of olive oil and a sprinkling of balsamic vinegar.

FOUR SERVINGS

3 tablespoons olive oil
1 small onion, thinly sliced
3 garlic cloves, minced
1 tablespoon tomato paste
1 cup dry white wine
3 ripe tomatoes, cut into large chunks
1 small eggplant, cut into 1-inch pieces
3 medium zucchini, cut into 1-inch pieces

1 red pepper, seeded and cut into thin strips
½ teaspoon thyme
1 bay leaf
Salt and freshly ground pepper to taste
2 tablespoon minced parsley
¼ cup shredded basil

Heat the olive oil in a large saucepan over medium-high heat. Add the onion slices and garlic; sauté until lightly golden, about 3 minutes. Add the tomato paste and cook, stirring for 2 minutes. Add the white wine and reduce by ½. Add the tomatoes and bring to a boil. Season with salt and cook for 3 minutes. Add the remaining vegetables, thyme and bay leaf. Cover, lower the heat to simmer and cook for 30 minutes.

Remove from the heat and stir in the parsley and basil. Adjust seasoning with salt and pepper and serve. This ratatouille can also be served at room temperature.

Grilled Asparagus

Asparagus are always delicious and a welcome addition to a meal, but a turn or two on the grill gives them a brand new appeal.

FOUR SERVINGS

1 bunch medium-size asparagus
2 tablespoons olive oil
Salt and freshly ground pepper to taste

1 tablespoon balsamic vinegar or more to taste
Thinly shaved Parmesan cheese (optional)

Preheat the grill to medium-high.

Snap off the tough ends of the asparagus stalks. Place the asparagus in a flat dish and drizzle with olive oil, salt and pepper. Rub all over to coat evenly.

Grill for about 8 minutes, turning once, until soft and lightly charred.

Place the asparagus on a serving platter and drizzle with the balsamic vinegar. Top with Parmesan shavings if desired. The asparagus can be served hot or at room temperature.

Brussels Sprouts and Potatoes en Papillote

MELISSA PERELLO

These papillotes can be assembled the day before and refrigerated until ready to grill. They can also be cooked in a 400° F oven.

TWO SERVINGS

2 small red new potatoes, sliced in ¼-inch pieces

1 cup Brussels sprouts, trimmed and split in ½

½ small yellow onion, thinly sliced

4 slices bacon, cut into small pieces

3 tablespoons olive oil

Preheat the grill to medium-high.

Blanch the potato slices for 1 minute in boiling salted water and cool. This will prevent the potatoes from discoloring.

Combine the potatoes, Brussels sprouts, onions and bacon in a mixing bowl. Toss in the olive oil and season with salt and pepper. Lay out 2 large sheets of aluminum foil and divide the vegetable mixture into 2 piles at the center of each. Pull up the sides and fold them into one another to tightly seal the packet.

Place packages on the grate of the grill. Cook on each side for about 4 to 5 minutes, rotating. Allow the packages to rest unopened for another 6 to 8 minutes. This will allow the vegetables to fully cook and meld the flavors together.

Chef
Melissa Perello

EXECUTIVE CHEF
Fifth Floor Restaurant, San Francisco

Climbing to the Top

Not long ago, at age 24, Melissa became one of the youngest executive chefs in the country. Smitten by her immense talent, local and national critics named her "the hottest chef in San Francisco and possibly the country." Today at the top of her game in her Fifth Floor Restaurant kitchen where she delivers French fare with a definite California attitude, she's still driven with the same strength and passion. She also carries these qualities along on her frequent backpacking trips in Northern California's outback.

Auspicious Beginnings

Some kids watch cartoons for entertainment, but Melissa preferred cooking shows. Julia Child was a favorite. That's how her mother found the pint-size 8-year-old Julia wannabe in the kitchen boning a leg of lamb.

Open Roads

Growing up in New Jersey, Melissa took frequent car camping trips with her family. Of course the limited amenities were not as deluxe as in your typical RV, but this family took meals seriously. A superb cook, her mother requested Melissa's dad build portable kitchen cupboards complete with drawers and shelf space to store dried herbs, ingredients and cooking equipment.

Trailing Along

Part of San Francisco's appeal for the energetic chef is the many options Northern California offers to backpacking enthusiasts. To get away from it all, Melissa seeks good trails her dog, Dingo, can also enjoy. Some of her favorite places to escape include the Shasta Trinity area, Kalamath River, Lost Coast and Big Sur.

Machine of Choice

In the early days, her hiking buddies loved to tease her about packing a lot of "heavy" food, to which she politely replied, "Well, I'm a chef, what do you expect?" Since then she has learned a few techniques and nifty tricks to lower her pack load, but still cooks up some great grub. One is her Excalibur food dehydrator. She uses it to dry vegetables like mushrooms, herbs, fruits and even fully finished dishes that can be packed and then re-hydrated at camp.

In Her Backpack:

Light packing means a quart-size Teflon pot with a lid and bottled water to revive her dehydrated dishes such as wild mushroom risotto.

Fifth Floor Restaurant

The Palomar Hotel
12 Fourth Street
San Francisco, CA 94103
415-348-1555
WWW.FIFTHFLOORRESTAURANT.COM

HIGH OCTANE
Desserts

Lemon Pound Cake

PATRICIA WILLIAMS

This versatile, moist and flavorful pound cake is the perfect traveling companion. Serve it at the end of a meal topped with grilled peaches or pan-roasted apple slices, or with a simple scoop of your favorite ice cream or a dollop of whipped cream. It is also delicious on its own as a mid-day snack or lightly toasted, spread with butter and jam for an easy breakfast.

MAKES 2 LOAVES

2 ⅓ cups cake flour
¾ teaspoon baking powder
Grated zest of 3 lemons
2 cups sugar
6 large eggs, room temperature
¾ cup crème fraîche or sour cream
3 ½ tablespoons brandy
3 tablespoons lemon juice
9 tablespoons melted butter, cooled
Pinch salt

GLAZE:
⅓ cup water
⅓ cup sugar
¼ cup lemon juice
Grated zest of 1 lemon

Preheat the oven to 350° F. Butter and flour two 8 ½ by 4 ½ by 2 ½ loaf pans.

In a large mixing bowl, combine the lemon zest with sugar. Add the eggs and whisk until the mixture is pale and foamy. Whisk in the crème fraîche (or sour cream), lemon juice, brandy and salt. Do not over mix or the cake will become tough.

Sift the flour and baking powder and fold into the egg mixture in thirds. Fold in the melted butter.

Pour the batter into the prepared loaf pans. Bake for 45 minutes or until the blade of a knife inserted into middle of the cake comes out clean. Unmold and cool on rack.

When the cakes are at room temperature, heat the water and sugar until the sugar is melted and the glaze is slightly thicker. Remove from the heat and add the lemon juice and zest. Drizzle the top and sides of the cakes with the glaze.

Chef
Patricia Williams

EXECUTIVE CHEF
District, New York City

Trailing Patricia

Before becoming one of the most accomplished female chefs in
Manhattan, Patricia was a professional ballerina with the New York
City Ballet. Upon retiring at the peak of her profession, she was
looking for a second career as challenging, creative and physical as the
one she was leaving behind. Little did she know that during a trip to
France to relax and get reacquainted with food, she would end up
working in a few kitchens and get hooked!

Women in the Kitchen

The self-taught chef apprenticed with some of New York's most
critically acclaimed chefs before developing her unique modern
American style and receiving her own recognition. Although she
arrived late into the biz, cooking wasn't new to Patricia. Part Cherokee
and part Mexican, she learned about the culture of food and women in
the kitchen at an early age as family members often got together for
days to cook for big celebrations.

Open Trails

Patricia has many childhood camping and RVing memories with family and friends. But her most memorable experience was riding the Salt Grass Trail Ride. The family took this horseback ride every year beginning in Brenham, Texas, and ending in Houston at the Live Stock auction. The family brought tents but also an RV. Harley, Patricia's father, would not dream of spending two weeks on the road without a shower!

Camp Food

"The meals were pretty simple but tasted great," recalls Patricia. They either emerged from the RV kitchen or were prepared on a campfire built in the dirt with a grate or a mock rotisserie. During the day, Harvey would disappear and reunite with the group a few hours later with freshly caught catfish, bass or trout to grill or cook wrapped in bacon in a well-used cast iron skillet, along with potatoes.

New Horizons

For years, Patricia pursued her interest in camping whenever she could, until she met the man she eventually married. This man sails! Now, during the boating season, you will find the couple on their sailboat on most weekends. "There is not too much difference," says Patricia, who has done it all. "It's about organization, knowing your menus and packing just what you need."

District
The Muse Hotel
130 West 46th Street
New York City, NY 10036
212-485-2999
WWW.DISTRICT-MUSEHOTEL.COM

Cherry Pie

CRAIG SHELTON

Craig's pie is not as sweet as most cherry pies; adjust the amount of sugar to your taste. If making pastry dough is not your forte, you could use two good quality ready-made frozen pie crusts.

SIX TO EIGHT SERVINGS

FILLING:
30 oz frozen unsweetened cherries
½ to ¾ cup sugar, to taste
2 tablespoons cornstarch
2 tablespoons lemon juice

PIE DOUGH:
2 ½ cups flour
¼ teaspoon salt
12 tablespoons cold butter or
    shortening cut into small dice
4 to 6 tablespoons iced water
1 beaten egg

Place the cherries in a colander set over a bowl and let them thaw.

Meanwhile, to make the crust, sift the flour and salt in a mixing bowl. Add the butter and using your finger tips or a pastry cutter, quickly blend into the flour until the mixture resembles coarse meal. Add the water 1 tablespoon at a time, until the dough just comes together. Do not over knead. This can be done in a food processor using the pulse function.

Gather the dough into a ball, halve the dough and roll each ½ into a ball. Flatten each ball into a thick disk, wrap in plastic wrap and refrigerate for at least 30 minutes.

Place the cherries in a mixing bowl, pour the reserved juices into a small saucepan and reduce over medium-low heat to ½ cup. Stir in the sugar, cornstarch and lemon juice. Stir the mixture into the cherries.

Preheat the oven to 375° F.

On lightly floured surface, roll out a disk of dough into an 11-inch circle. Line a 9-inch pie plate with the dough, leaving ¾-inch overhang. Spoon the cherry mixture into the crust.

Roll out the 2nd disk into a 13-inch circle. Cut out a small hole at the center. Arrange the dough over the filling. Seal by pressing along the edges. Trim the double overhang to ¾-inch. Fold under and crimp the edges of the pie. Brush the top crust with the beaten egg.

Place the pie on a cookie sheet and bake for 50 minutes to 1 hour until the crust is golden brown. Remove from the oven and cool on rack.

Panettone Bread Pudding

PRISCILLA MARTEL

Bread pudding is the ultimate comfort food. Priscilla's recipe is a sophisticated interpretation of the white bread nursery version. Panettone is the traditional Italian Christmas sweet bread that is now available year round. It is delicious with just a smear of butter or turned into succulent creations such as golden French toast or this delicious pudding. If you don't have panettone on hand, substitute with commercial raisin bread.

SIX TO EIGHT SERVINGS

Butter for greasing baking dish
½ cup heavy cream
2 cups milk
⅓ cup sugar
Pinch of salt
2 eggs

1 lb panettone such as Motta,
     cut into 2-inch cubes
2 to 3 thin slices panettone (optional)
Whipped cream for garnish
Caramel sauce or brandy syrup for
     garnish

Preheat the oven to 350° F. Butter a 9 x 12-inch baking dish with 2 to 3 tablespoons butter. Set aside.

Combine the cream, milk, sugar, salt and eggs in a large bowl. Beat until the mixture is well blended.

Add the cubed panettone, stirring so all of the bread is moistened with the custard. Let set for 30 minutes.

Spoon the custard-soaked panettone into the prepared pan. Place thin slices of panettone over the top of the custard, if desired. This will give the finished pudding a more uniform surface.

Bake the panettone until evenly browned and the custard is set, about 1 hour.

Cool for 15 minutes before serving. Slice and serve with unsweetened whipped cream and a drizzle of caramel sauce or brandy syrup.

TIP   Layering thin slices of panettone over the top of the custard will give a more elegant uniform surface to the finished pudding.

Free-Form Apple-Pear Tart with Cider Syrup

DANIEL BRUCE

This rustic apple tart with a flaky buttery crust doesn't require a special mold or fancy design. The reduced cider drizzled at the end intensifies the flavor of the fruit and adds a nice caramel edge. Serve it warm with a scoop of vanilla ice cream.

SIX SERVINGS

1 cup flour
3 teaspoons sugar
Pinch of salt
6 tablespoons butter, chilled and cut into small dice
2 tablespoons shortening, chilled and cut into small dice
3 to 4 tablespoons iced water
¼ teaspoon nutmeg

¼ teaspoon cinnamon
1 teaspoon cornstarch diluted in ¼ cup water
1 ripe Comice pear or other variety, cored, peeled and sliced
1 tart green apple, cored, peeled and sliced
2 cups apple cider

Combine the flour, 1 teaspoon sugar and salt in a mixing bowl. Add 4 tablespoons butter and the shortening to the bowl; using your finger tips or a pastry cutter, quickly blend into the flour until the mixture resembles coarse meal with some small butter pieces remaining. This will result in a flakier crust. Add the water 1 tablespoon at a time until the dough just comes together; do not over knead. This can be done in a food processor using the pulse function. Form the dough into a ball, wrap in plastic wrap and refrigerate for at least 30 minutes.

Melt the remaining butter in a skillet over medium-high heat. Add the apple and pear slices and toss to coat. Sprinkle with the cinnamon, nutmeg and remaining sugar and cook, stirring until the fruit starts to soften, about 2 minutes. Stir in the cornstarch and water mixture and simmer for 1 minute. Remove from the heat and cool.

Preheat oven to 375° F. Butter a cookie sheet.

Place the dough on a lightly floured work surface. Roll out into a circle about 9-inch diameter. Do not worry if the circle or the edges are not perfect. Place the dough on the prepared cookie sheet. Spread the filling at the center, leaving a 1½ to 2 inch border all around. Fold the border over the filling, leaving the center open face. Bake for 35 to 40 minutes.

Meanwhile, place the cider in a small stainless steel saucepan and reduce to about ¾ to ½ cup, to a syrup consistency. Remove from the heat and cool slightly.

Remove the tart from the oven and cool for 3 to 4 minutes. Drizzle the cider syrup all over the filling and serve immediately.

TIP Many fruits are well-suited for this no-frill tart, especially ripe apricots, peaches and plums or any combination. Instead of reducing cider, melt some apricot jam with 1 to 2 tablespoons of brandy and drizzle over the warm tart. You can also toss 1 to 2 tablespoons finely chopped almonds or walnuts into the fruit filling just before baking.

The dough is a perfect foil to many savory fillings. Here is a suggestion: Spread some Dijon mustard on the dough. Layer with thinly sliced fresh tomato and season with salt and pepper. Sprinkle with fresh thyme, grated Swiss cheese, and a drizzle of olive oil.

Although there is nothing like flaky buttery homemade dough, in a pinch you can use store-bought frozen puff pastry. Thaw the dough before using.

Boston Harbor Hotel
Daniel Bruce

Chef
Daniel Bruce

EXECUTIVE CHEF
*Boston Harbor Hotel and
Meritage Restaurant, Boston*

Trailing Daniel

A native New Englander, Daniel is the executive chef of the prestigious Boston Harbor Hotel, where he oversees three dining venues including the critically acclaimed Meritage Restaurant. Fresh out of Johnson & Wales in Rhode Island, the young chef sharpened his skills under the watchful eyes of culinary masters in Italy and France as well as New York City, eventually becoming the executive chef of the legendary "21" Club in Manhattan. As one of the country's most promising young chefs, his beloved New England lured Bruce back. He eventually opened his dream restaurant Meritage where he combines his passion for wine and food. Daniel also created the enormously popular Boston Wine Festival.

Backwoods Boy

He grew up in rural Maine, the son of a registered hunting-and-fishing guide, in a three-room house with very few modern amenities. And the nearest neighbor was 15 miles away. Food and the gathering of it was the center of much of his daily life. Besides the bountiful garden, the family foraged for wild edibles such as mushrooms and fiddlehead ferns and caught fish in nearby streams and lakes. "Food was a communal thing. That's what got me interested," recalls the chef. "My grandmother canned the vegetables from the garden and made pies from scratch. My mother was a very good cook, too."

Wild Cuisine

Although he now travels in the glamorous world of food and wine, Daniel often looks to his humble roots for inspiration on his outstanding menus—and occasionally goes wild! Very aware of the cycle of the seasons and the food that grows around him, he showcases local produce as much as possible, buying from small local farmers and foragers.

Different Kind of Camp

For a couple of weeks every summer, the Bruce family heads up to a camp in Maine where life is as rustic as he remembers his childhood. The small cabin has an old-fashioned wood stove and no television or computer games to distract from the beauty of the surroundings. Reconnecting with nature, the family spends most of their time reading, hiking, fishing and gathering food. Daniel passionately believes that this time away getting back to nature is an important contribution to his children's education.

In His Coolers:

When preparing for his annual trip, Daniel packs mostly staples, as he prefers buying fresh produce from farm stands and picking his own wild mushrooms and other delicacies such as summer berries along the way. A word of caution: foraging is not for everyone. Unless you have years of experience and have trained with an expert, stick to farm stands and supermarkets.

Meritage Restaurant

Boston Harbor Hotel
70 Rowes Wharf
Boston, MA 02110
617-439-3995
WWW.MERITAGETHERESTAURANT.COM

Native Strawberry-Rhubarb Shortcakes with Vermont Maple Syrup Mascarpone

DANIEL BRUCE

One of the great pleasures of discovering a region, especially if you are a chef, is through its local produce. This dessert is about the flavors of New England, but that should not stop you from trying it wherever you have parked for the night.

SIX TO EIGHT SERVINGS

SHORTCAKES:
- 1 cup sifted all-purpose flour
- 1 tablespoon baking powder
- 3 tablespoons granulated sugar
- 8 tablespoons cold butter, cut into ¼-inch cubes
- 1 teaspoon vanilla
- 1 egg, beaten
- ¼ cup milk

FILLING:
- ½ lb rhubarb stalks, rinsed and cut into small cubes
- ½ cup sugar
- 1 pt strawberries, rinsed and hulled
- 1 cup Vermont mascarpone (or imported)
- ¼ cup Vermont or pure maple syrup
- Powdered sugar and mint sprigs for garnish

Preheat the oven to 350° F. Butter and lightly flour a cookie sheet.

Combine all the dry ingredients for the shortcake in a mixing bowl. Add the butter to the bowl and blend, using a pastry cutter or finger tips, until the mixture resembles coarse meal.

Combine the milk, egg and vanilla in a small mixing bowl. Pour into the flour mixture, stirring until just incorporated into the dough; do not over mix as the shortcake will become less flaky.

Turn the dough out onto a lightly floured work surface and roll out to 1-inch thick. Cut into four 3-inch circles, using a cookie cutter or the rim of a glass. Place the dough on the prepared cookie sheet and bake for 15 minutes, or until the shortcakes are golden brown. Remove from the oven and cool.

Meanwhile, combine the rhubarb and sugar in a saucepan and simmer over medium heat for 5 minutes until tender. Remove from the heat and add to a mixing bowl.

Quarter the strawberries and toss with the rhubarb mixture. Set aside for 30 minutes to develop flavors.

In a mixing bowl, combine the mascarpone and maple syrup and whisk to a soft peak.

When ready to serve, halve the shortcakes crosswise. Spoon the strawberry-rhubarb mixture onto each shortcake bottom and top with a dollop of mascarpone. Cover with the remaining tops. Lightly dust with powdered sugar and garnish with a sprig of mint.

Apple Crumble

JIMMY BANNOS

Jimmy's crumble can be assembled the day before and kept refrigerated until ready to bake. This great easy dessert will become a favorite, especially when served alongside a scoop of ice cream or topped with whipped cream. Leftovers are delicious cold the next day.

FOUR SERVINGS

4 large apples, cored and cut into 1-inch chunks
½ cup granulated sugar
2 tablespoons lemon juice
1 teaspoon ground cinnamon
½ cup rolled oats
½ cup brown sugar

4 tablespoons chilled butter, cut into cubes
⅓ cup chopped nuts such as walnuts or pecans
Ice cream, frozen yogurt or whipped cream, optional

Preheat the grill to medium.

Combine the apples, granulated sugar, lemon juice and ½ teaspoon cinnamon in a disposable 8 x 8-inch aluminum foil pan. Stir well to blend.

In a small bowl, combine the oats, brown sugar, nuts and remaining cinnamon. Cut in the butter, working with a fork or fingertips until the mixture is crumbly. Sprinkle the mixture evenly over the apples. Cover the pan tightly with aluminum foil and cook on the grill until bubbly, about 15 to 20 minutes.

Remove from the grill and let sit for several minutes before serving. Carefully remove the foil and serve with ice cream, frozen yogurt or whipped cream, if desired.

Warm Cherry Crisp

MINUTEMEALS CHEFS

Here is a snappy yet sumptuous dessert that doesn't require any special equipment or technique. For the topping you may use your preferred store-bought granola or make a batch of Cynthia Keller's on page 20. As a variation, you may use any of your favorite pie fillings. Dried sour cherries are a real treat and are frequently sold in small bags in the produce section of large supermarkets. Use them as you would raisins.

FOUR SERVINGS

One 21 oz can cherry pie filling
½ cup dried sour cherries, raisins or chopped dried apricots
½ teaspoon ground cinnamon

2 tablespoons butter, melted
3 cups granola, homemade (see recipe on page 20) or store-bought
1 pt vanilla ice cream (optional)

Preheat the oven to 350° F.

In a medium saucepan, combine the cherry pie filling, dried cherries and cinnamon. Bring to a boil over medium heat, stirring constantly.

Combine the granola and melted butter in a small mixing bowl. Pat ½ the granola mixture into a 9 ¼ by 6 ½ by 2-inch baking pan. Place the pan in the oven and bake for 5 minutes until the layer begins to brown.

Spoon the hot cherry filling over the toasted granola crust and top it with the remaining granola mixture. Return the pan to the oven and bake until the topping browns, about 10 minutes. Serve warm with vanilla ice cream, if desired.

Adapted from Minutemeals.com

Pear Clafouti

Clafouti is a very versatile rustic fruit gratin traditionally prepared with fresh black cherries. In this recipe, we are using pears for a late-summer and fall dessert, but you could also use apples or any stone-fruits such as plums and apricots according to seasonal availability. Raspberries and blueberries are also good substitutes; increase the amount of flour by ½ cup to compensate for the extra juice. Don't worry about leftovers—clafouti is a wonderful breakfast treat.

SIX TO EIGHT SERVINGS

¾ cup milk
¾ cup heavy cream
½ cup sugar
3 large eggs
⅔ cup sifted flour
1 teaspoon vanilla extract

Pinch of salt
3 cups peeled and thinly sliced pears.
  2 to 3 pears depending on size,
  preferably Anjou, Bartlett or Bosc
3 tablespoons confectioner's sugar
(optional)

Preheat the oven to 350° F. Lightly butter a 9-inch baking dish.

In a mixing bowl, whisk together the milk, heavy cream, sugar, eggs, flour, vanilla extract and salt. Beat the mixture to a smooth batter. This can be done in a blender or food processor.

Spread a ½-inch layer of batter into the prepared dish, stilting to evenly coat the bottom. Spread the pear slices over the batter, pour on the remaining batter and smooth the top.

Bake the clafouti for 45 to 50 minutes until puffed and golden and the tip of a knife inserted in the center comes out clean. Remove from the oven and dust with confectioner's sugar (optional). The clafouti can be served hot or warm with pear sorbet or vanilla ice cream.

Pineapple and Coconut Sheet Cake

This cake is a crowd pleaser that can be served as a dessert or a mid-afternoon snack with a cup of coffee. It will stay moist for up to 3 days—that is if you can keep it that long!

EIGHT TO TEN SERVINGS

Butter for greasing the pan
2 cups flour
1 ¼ cups sugar
1 teaspoon baking soda
2 large eggs, beaten
½ cup vegetable oil
½ teaspoon vanilla extract
One 20 oz can crushed pineapple

ICING:
1 cup sugar
⅔ cup evaporated milk
½ cup butter
1 cup chopped nuts
1 cup shredded coconut

Preheat the oven to 350° F. Butter the bottom and sides of a sheet pan.

Combine the flour, sugar and baking soda in a mixing bowl. In another bowl, beat the eggs, oil and vanilla extract until well combined. Fold in the pineapple.

Pour the mixture into the prepared sheet cake pan and bake for 20 to 30 minutes.

Meanwhile, prepare the icing. Place the sugar, milk and butter in a small saucepan and bring to a boil. Lower the heat to simmer and cook, stirring constantly for about 10 minutes until the mixture thickens. Remove from the heat and stir in the nuts and coconut.

Remove the cake from the oven and put the icing on top while still hot. Cool to room temperature before serving.

Summer Melons with Fresh Mint, Vanilla Crème Fraîche

NEAL FRASER

The revival of heirloom foods is a welcome trend slowly taking hold around the country. This simple dessert is an illustration of less is more when it comes to flavors. Use the recipe as a guideline and adapt it to what you'll find in your travels, as long as the selected fruits are at the peak of their ripeness. Lately some of these suggested melons have been appearing in supermarkets, but if you can find them locally, grab them. In any case, select 2 different kinds for contrasting texture and color.

SIX SERVINGS

1 vanilla bean
¾ cup crème fraîche or whipping cream, chilled
2 tablespoons sugar
2 small heirloom melons: Charentais, Amarillo Oro, Ananas, Persian or other types available at the market

1 small bunch regular mint, Turkish mint or Shiso leaves, finely shredded

Halve the vanilla bean and using the tip of a knife, scrape the seeds and place them in a mixing bowl.

Add the crème fraîche or whipping cream and sugar to the bowl. Whip the mixture to stiff peaks and refrigerate until ready to serve.

Halve the melons and discard the seeds. Cut into wedges and separate the rind from the flesh. Cut the melons into bite-size pieces. Divide the melon among 6 serving plates, top with a generous dollop of whipped cream and garnish with the shredded mint.

Grilled Peaches

PATRICIA WILLIAMS

For best results, select ripe peaches that are firm and unblemished.

FOUR SERVINGS

2 large peaches
2 tablespoons melted butter
4 thick slices lemon pound cake
  (recipe on page 161)

Preheat the grill to medium-high.

Quarter the peaches and place into a shallow dish. Toss with melted butter to evenly coat on all sides.

Place the peaches on the grill and cook for a couple of minutes on each side until just soft and lightly caramelized. Serve with crème fraîche, whipped cream, ice cream or yogurt on top of the lemon pound cake.

Grilled Pineapple-Peach Kabobs

JIMMY BANNOS

Jimmy's basting sauce gives a wonderful caramel edge with a hint of spiciness to these grilled fruit kabobs. Feel free to experiment with other fruits.

FOUR SERVINGS

8 skewers
Four ¾-inch thick slices fresh
   pineapple, each cut into 6 wedges,
   excess juice reserved
2 large ripe but firm peaches,
   pitted and cut into 8 wedges

4 tablespoons butter
1 teaspoon minced, seeded jalapeño
   chile
⅛ teaspoon ground black pepper
3 tablespoons brown sugar
2 tablespoons lime juice

Soak the bamboo skewers in cold water for 1 hour before using. This is to keep them from catching fire when placed over the hot fire.

Heat the grill to medium-high.

Alternately thread 3 pieces pineapple and 2 pieces peach onto each skewer.

Melt the butter in a small saucepan, add the jalapeño and black pepper and simmer for 2 minutes. Brush the mixture on the fruit. Mix the remaining half butter with the brown sugar, lime juice and 1 to 2 tablespoons of the reserved pineapple juice until the sugar is dissolved.

Grill the fruit kabobs for 3 to 4 minutes, turning occasionally to evenly roast. Baste with the butter and brown sugar mixture and cook for an additional 2 minutes. Remove from the grill, baste with any remaining butter mixture and serve warm.

Pan-Roasted Caramelized Apples

CHARLIE PALMER

This is an easy dessert that works equally well at a campsite, in an RV kitchen or at home. If you have pound cake or another plain cake on hand, slice it and toast it on the grill for an even more flavorful dessert. You can also add 3 tablespoons raisins or currants, or 2 tablespoons walnuts or pecans as well as 1 to 2 tablespoons rum or brandy to the basic recipe. You could also add all of them for a very fancy dessert.

FOUR SERVINGS

2 tablespoons butter
⅓ cup light brown sugar
½ teaspoon ground cinnamon
4 medium firm tart apples, peeled, cored and cut lengthwise into thick slices

If using a grill, heat until hot.

Place a cast iron or heavy gauge skillet on the grate of the grill or over low heat on the stove top. When hot, add the butter, stirring to melt. Add the sugar and cinnamon, stirring to blend. When nicely combined, add the apple slices and cook over low heat, stirring occasionally for about 20 minutes or until the apples are nicely caramelized.

Remove from the heat and serve hot over ice cream, frozen yogurt or slices of plain cake or straight from the pan with a dollop of whipped cream.

Almond Panna Cotta with Native Peaches

JAMIE RORABACK

Panna cotta (cooked cream) is a delicate custard dessert from Northern Italy. It is traditionally made with simmered cream, sugar and gelatin and served with a fresh fruit puree. In this recipe, Jamie created a lighter version, using milk instead of cream and adding a generous splash of almond liqueur, Amaretto, for flavoring. Once you have mastered the technique, you could easily experiment with other flavors. For an alcohol-free dessert substitute the Amaretto with 1 teaspoon vanilla extract or better yet, vanilla seeds scraped from half a pod.

SIX SERVINGS

3 tablespoons Amaretto
1 ½ teaspoons unflavored gelatin
2 cups milk
¾ cup sugar
2 peaches, peeled and cut into ½-inch dice

1 teaspoon freshly squeezed lemon juice
Fresh peach slices, mint leaves, toasted almonds and crisp cookies for garnish

Place the Amaretto in a small mixing bowl, and sprinkle with the gelatin. Set aside for 5 to 10 minutes until the gelatin softens.

In a small saucepan, combine ½ cup sugar with the milk and bring to a simmer. Remove from heat. Add the softened gelatin and Amaretto mixture, stirring until completely dissolved.

Divide the mixture into six 4 oz molds, ramekins or glasses and refrigerate for at least 2 hours or until firm.

Meanwhile, combine the diced peaches with the remaining sugar and the lemon juice. Refrigerate until ready to serve.

To serve, spoon some of the marinated peaches atop the panna cotta.

For a more elegant dessert, briefly dip the molds in hot water to loosen the custard and invert onto individual dessert plates. Surround each panna cotta with the peaches. Garnish with few fresh peach slices, mint leaves, toasted almonds and a crisp cookie.

Simple, Rich and Light Chocolate Mousse

JAMIE RORABACK

This mousse is basically a soft ganache that is chilled and lightly whipped. It is both rich and light! And best of all, it can be made according to your chocoholic cravings, using dark, milk or white chocolate. For best results, the cocoa content of the selected chocolate should not exceed 58%.

SIX SERVINGS

7 oz chocolate, semisweet, milk, or white, coarsely chopped
1 ¼ cups heavy cream
1 tablespoon butter
1 tablespoon sugar

1 tablespoon liqueur such as Grand Marnier, Chambord, or Kahlua (optional)
Fresh fruit, cookies, mint leaves for garnish

Place the chocolate in a mixing bowl.

In saucepan, combine the heavy cream, butter and sugar. Bring just to a boil, stirring to melt the butter. Pour the mixture over the chopped chocolate. Add the liqueur (optional) and stir until the chocolate is melted and the mixture smooth.

Refrigerate the mixture for at least 3 hours or overnight.

When ready to serve, whip the mixture with a hand whisk to medium peaks. The mousse should be slightly firm and have an airy consistency. Do not over whip, otherwise the mousse will become grainy. Serve with fresh fruit, crisp cookies and garnish with a mint leaf.

Connecticut Pure Maple Mousse

JAMIE RORABACK

This is a very easy and elegant dessert. Obviously, Jamie is a little chauvinistic while recommending his home state sweet gold, but any origin is fine as long as you use PURE maple syrup.

SIX SERVINGS

4 teaspoons cold water
1 teaspoon plain gelatin
1 cup heavy cream, chilled
¼ cup egg whites

¼ cup pure maple syrup
Whipped cream and cookies for
  garnish

Place the water in a small mixing bowl, sprinkle in the gelatin and set aside for 5 to 10 minutes, until the gelatin softens.

Meanwhile, whip the heavy cream to a soft peak. Refrigerate until ready to use.

Place the egg whites and maple syrup in a mixing bowl. Set the bowl over a pot of simmering water and whip until the mixture is frosty and warmed. Remove from heat.

Using an electric mixer, whip the mixture to soft peaks. Add the gelatin and whip until well combined. Gently fold in the whipped cream, using a rubber spatula, until no white streaks remain. Pour the mixture into serving glasses or molds and chill for at least 1 hour before serving. Serve with whipped cream and crisp cookies.

Chocolate Brownie Ice-Cream Sandwiches

These cookies are drier than and not as fudgy as the average brownie, but they pack a lot of flavors and are delicious eaten on their own. They can be prepared ahead and kept frozen for up to 1 month.

MAKES 12 COOKIES

8 tablespoons butter, softened, plus some for greasing the pan
4 oz bittersweet chocolate, coarsely chopped
¾ cup flour
½ teaspoon baking powder
Pinch of salt

¼ teaspoon cinnamon
½ cup sugar
2 large eggs
1 teaspoon vanilla extract
½ cup finely chopped walnuts
1 pt vanilla ice cream or any of your favorite flavors

Preheat the oven to 375° F. Butter 2 cookie sheets.

Melt the chocolate in a bowl set over simmering water, stirring once in a while. Set aside to cool.

Combine the flour, baking powder, salt and cinnamon in a mixing bowl. Place the butter, sugar and vanilla in another mixing bowl and whip until the mixture is smooth and well incorporated. Add the eggs and blend to combine. Stir in the chocolate and the flour mixture. Fold in the walnuts.

Drop heaping tablespoons of batter onto the prepared cookie sheets. Gently flatten the top to form rounds about 2 inches in diameter.

Bake for 7 to 8 minutes until the exterior is dried but the brownies are soft to the touch. Remove from the oven and cool. Loosen the brownies from the cookie sheets and refrigerate until ready to serve.

To serve: spread a thick layer of ice cream on 1 brownie and top with another.

Hot Fudge Sauce

MINUTEMEALS CHEFS

Most recipes for hot fudge sauce use white sugar and water. The Minutemeals chefs upped the ante and substituted dark brown sugar and cream, which gives this sauce a hint of caramel flavor and a beautiful shiny appearance.

FOUR SERVINGS

2 tablespoons butter

2 squares (2 oz) unsweetened
  chocolate, coarsely chopped

¾ cup firmly packed dark brown sugar

2 tablespoons light corn syrup

½ cup heavy cream

½ teaspoon pure vanilla extract

Note: You can store leftovers right in the glass measuring cup for up to 2 weeks. Simply cover the cooled sauce with plastic wrap and chill. To reheat the sauce, unwrap and set the measuring cup in a saucepan with a few inches of simmering water. Carefully stir it as it softens.

Melt the butter over low heat in a small saucepan. Add the chocolate and melt, stirring occasionally, until the butter and chocolate are well blended. Remove the pan from the heat.

Quickly add the sugar and whisk to dissolve any lumps and until the mixture is smooth and shiny. Return the pan over low heat and bring to a simmer. Stir in the corn syrup and heavy cream and simmer for 7 to 9 minutes without stirring. The longer you cook it, the chewier it will become.

Pour the sauce into a bowl and stir in the ½ teaspoon vanilla extract along with any of the optional flavorings. Serve over ice cream or frozen yogurt.

Adapted from Minutemeals.com

Variations:

For Mexican Hot Fudge Sauce: add ¾ teaspoon ground cinnamon
For Adult Hot Fudge Sauce: add 1 tablespoon rum (or to taste)
For Mandarin Orange Hot Fudge Sauce: add 2 strips of orange zest. Remove before serving.

8

Stow

In this chapter you will find a selection of miscellaneous recipes that are easy to assemble in a snap or can be prepared a few days or weeks before your scheduled departure and stored in your cupboard, freezer or refrigerator. Use them in a pinch for no-brainer sauces, marinades or rubs, or to lend some kick to all manners of vegetables and meats.

Balsamic Vinegar Marinade

CHARLIE PALMER

This tasty marinade yields enough for 1 ½ pounds meat, poultry or fish. Refrigerate until ready to use.

MAKES ABOUT ¾ CUP

½ cup balsamic vinegar
3 tablespoons olive oil
1 tablespoon orange juice concentrate
1 tablespoon minced shallots

1 teaspoon dried thyme
½ teaspoon freshly ground pepper
Coarse salt to taste

Mix all of the ingredients together. Cover tightly and keep refrigerated for up to 2 weeks or frozen up to 1 month.

When ready to use, place the poultry, meat or fish to be marinated in a shallow glass baking pan. Pour the marinade over the top and, using tongs, turn to coat all sides. Cover with plastic film and refrigerate for about 2 hours.

Remove from the refrigerator, uncover and shake each piece gently to allow excess marinade to drip off. Season with salt to taste. Grill, roast or pan fry as you desire.

The Art of the Marinade

When using marinades, make sure the meat is completely covered.

Allow enough time for the meats to absorb the marinade. Tender meats like filet mignon only need 1 to 2 hours for marinating. Meats that are tougher should be given more time, ranging from 3 to 4 hours or overnight in order for the meat to become more flavorful.

Always marinade meats in the refrigerator. Never leave meats in a marinade unrefrigerated for more than few minutes before cooking. Meats that have been frozen in a marinade should be thawed in the refrigerator.

Meats should only be marinated in glass, plastic bowls or sealed bags. Never use a metal bowl or container; the acidity in the marinade will cause oxidation and spoil the meat.

Marinades should never be reused because of bacteria that may have developed or is present from the previous meat used.

—Frank Ottomanelli

Asian Marinade

CHARLIE PALMER

This tasty marinade yields enough for 1 ½ pounds meat, poultry or fish. Refrigerate until ready to use.

MAKES ABOUT 1 CUP

½ cup soy sauce
3 tablespoons grape seed or other
    mild vegetable oil
2 teaspoons orange juice
2 tablespoons minced fresh ginger

2 tablespoons minced scallions,
    including some green part
1 teaspoon minced garlic
½ teaspoon red chili flakes or to taste
Freshly ground pepper to taste
Coarse salt to taste

Combine the soy sauce, oil and juice in a small bowl, whisking to blend. Stir in the ginger, scallions, garlic, chili flakes and pepper.

Place the meat or poultry to be marinated in a shallow glass baking pan. Pour the marinade over the top and, using tongs, turn to coat all sides. Cover with plastic film and refrigerate for about 2 hours.

Remove from the refrigerator, uncover and shake each piece gently to allow excess marinade to drip off. Season with salt to taste. Grill, roast or pan fry as you desire

Dry Spice Rub

CHARLIE PALMER

This great all-around spice rub yields enough for 4 pounds poultry, meat or fish. Store it in an airtight container for up to 1 month.

MAKES ABOUT 3 TABLESPOONS

2 teaspoons ground cumin
2 teaspoons curry powder
1 teaspoon ground cinnamon

1 teaspoon ground white pepper
1 teaspoon brown sugar
1 teaspoon coarse salt

Combine all of the ingredients in a small bowl. Use immediately or cover tightly and store in a cool, dark spot for up to 1 month. When ready to use, rub a generous coating of the spice mixture onto the skin of poultry or fish. Grill or roast as you desire.

Toasted Jalapeño Tomatillo and Watermelon Salsa

CHEF HARRY

This salsa can be kept refrigerated for up to 3 days. Serve it as a dip or spoon over Lobster and Goat Cheese Quesadillas (on page 30), or any grilled meats, poultry or fish.

MAKES ABOUT 3 CUPS

8 to 10 medium tomatillos
2 tablespoons vegetable oil
1 onion, minced
2 garlic cloves, minced
3 jalapeño peppers, seeded and
   chopped, or to taste

1 tablespoon ground cumin
2 teaspoons mild chili powder
1 cup tomato sauce or puree
1 cup seeded watermelon, cut into
   1-inch cubes
Salt and freshly ground pepper
   to taste

Peel off the tomatillos' parchment-like skin and rinse under cold running water. Cut the tomatillos into quarters.

Heat the oil in a large heavy skillet over medium-high heat. Add the onions and sauté for 2 to 3 minutes. Add the tomatillos, garlic and jalapeños and cook until the onions and garlic begin to brown.

Reduce the heat to low, sprinkle with the cumin and chili powder, stir in the tomato sauce and bring to a simmer. Remove from heat and cool.

Place the mixture in the bowl of a food processor or blender along with the watermelon. Puree until smooth. Season with salt and pepper to taste and refrigerate until ready to serve.

TIP Tomatillo is a fruit that looks like a small green tomato wrapped into a parchment-like husk. It has a tart citrus flavor and is eaten raw, diced into salsas or cooked in sauces and stir-frys. Tomatillos will keep refrigerated for up to 2 weeks and may be frozen.

Chef Harry

TV PERSONALITY AND BOOK AUTHOR

When Things Get Harry

On the Shop at Home Network, the energetic chef hosts *Kitchen Corner*, showcasing everything you could every want for that much-used room—including the kitchen sink. He also hosts *Chef Harry & Friends* on PBS, based on his latest book *The Fit Foundation: A Guide to Help Achieve Good Health For America's Overweight Youth*. Get inspired as he invites himself into homes around the country and provides health makeovers.

Hooked on the Roaming Lifestyle

As a 17-year old teenager, Chef Harry was introduced to, and instantly seduced by, the nomadic lifestyle while traveling as an owner and exhibitor to national horse shows. Self-described cheesecake addicts, he and his trainer selected their dining venues by the availability of the dessert. (He has since reformed!) And at potluck dinners shared with fellow horsemen, his Reuben sandwich sealed his reputation as a great cook.

15,000 Miles of Open Road

While most of us love RVing for leisure, Chef Harry travels on wheels for business. His "Rock & Roll" state-of-the-art 40-foot bus boasts indoor and outdoor kitchens for entertaining, a high-tech entertainment center, personal office space and deluxe amenities. Avoiding hopping from plane to plane is a major draw, but luxury for Chef Harry is the ability to bring his family and dog along on his adventures.

Roadside Entertaining

Greatly influenced by his mother's lavish, over-the-top home entertaining, he loves to throw a party whenever possible. Fifty people for lunch at a camp resort? No problem. He whipped up watermelon salsa, grilled shrimp tandoori and assorted side dishes in no time.

Memorable Stops

Chef Harry has had his share of overnighters parked at soulless truck stops. Those were memorable! On the fun side, he enjoyed Disney's Fort Wilderness Resort & Campground for its privacy and user-friendly amenities and Asheville, North Carolina for its fresh and colorful farmer's market.

In His Pantry:

You'll find Wolfgang Puck canned soups, herb infused oils and vinegars, assorted relishes picked up along the way at various local markets, dried herbs and spices and cream cheese.

Book Stash:

Fit Foundation: A Guide to Help Achieve Good Health for America's Overweight Youth by Chef Harry (Volt Press, 2006).

Star Grazing by Chef Harry (Volt Press, 2001).

To find out where Chef Harry will be next, www.chefharry.com.

Mango-Lemon Salsa

CHEF HARRY

Serve this chunky salsa with blue corn chips or spoon over just about anything that comes off the grill. It is especially delicious with grilled salmon and chicken. The salsa will keep refrigerated for up to 2 days.

MAKES 3 TO 4 CUPS, ABOUT EIGHT SERVINGS

1 to 2 firm but ripe mangos
Juice of 4 lemons
½ cup chopped cilantro
1 small red onion, minced
1 jalapeño pepper, seeded and
  minced

2 small tomatoes, seeded and
  chopped
1 tablespoon poppy seed
Salt and freshly ground pepper to
  taste

Peel the mangos and cut the flesh into small dice. Drizzle with the lemon juice and toss to coat.

Add the cilantro, onion, jalapeño pepper, tomatoes and poppy seed. Stir well to blend and season with salt and pepper to taste. Serve cold or at room temperature.

TIP   For a flavorful and healthy meal, grill some salmon filets and place over organic baby greens. Spoon the salsa lavishly over the fish and serve hot or at room temperature.

Cocktail Hour
Watermelon Coconut Daiquiri

Whip up a couple batches of *Chef Harry's* colorful concoction and invite your new next door neighbors over for hors d'oeuvres. The festive daiquiri is the perfect match for some of the spicy salsas scattered throughout the book.

ONE SERVING

2 cups seeded watermelon chunks
2 oz coconut flavored rum
½ cup shredded coconut
Juice from 1 fresh lime
1 cup ice

Place all ingredients in a blender and blend until smooth. Pour into a sugar rimmed glass.

Corn and Black Bean Salsa

CHEF HARRY

This colorful salsa will keep refrigerated for up to 3 days. Serve with chips or grilled poultry, meats or fish.

MAKES 4 CUPS, ABOUT SIX TO EIGHT SERVINGS

2 cups fresh corn kernels or canned
Juice of 4 limes
1 mild green chili pepper, seeded and minced
1 jalapeño pepper, seeded and minced (optional)
1 teaspoon chili powder

1 teaspoon ground cumin
1 small onion, minced
2 garlic cloves, minced
Chopped fresh cilantro, to taste
1 teaspoon granulated sugar
1 can (15 oz) prepared black beans, rinsed and drained

If using canned corn, drain and rinse the kernels. If using fresh corn, boil the kernels in lightly salted water for 5 minutes. Drain and cool.

Place the corn kernels in a glass bowl and stir in all of the ingredients except the beans. Fold the beans gently into the salsa at the end. Cover and refrigerate until ready to serve.

TIP If you find yourself with any leftover salsa, drain and combine with shredded cheddar. Spoon the mixture onto a tortilla and toast in a skillet or on a griddle until the mixture is hot and the cheese melted.

Papaya Salsa

CHEF HARRY

Serve this zesty fruity salsa with grilled or pan-sautéed fish filets. It will keep refrigerated for up to 2 days.

MAKES ABOUT 1 CUP

1 cup papaya (reserve the seeds if desired and use as seasoning in the salsa)
Juice of 3 medium limes
½ cup chopped, seeded tomato

½ cup chopped cilantro
¼ cup minced white onion
1 teaspoon sugar
1 teaspoon cumin

Combine all the ingredients in a glass bowl and stir until well blended. Refrigerate for at least 1 to 2 hours before serving to allow the flavors to blend.

TIP   Papaya seeds are edible and very peppery. Grind a few in a salad dressing for a burst of fruity spice flavor.

Basic Vinaigrette

This reliable all-around vinaigrette can be kept refrigerated in a jar for 1 to 2 weeks. It will equally dress delicate leafy greens and sturdier vegetable or meat salads. Shake well before using.

MAKES 1½ CUPS

2 tablespoons Dijon mustard
Salt and freshly ground black pepper to taste

6 tablespoons red wine vinegar
1 cup olive oil
½ cup vegetable oil

Place all the ingredients in a covered jar and shake well to blend. Adjust seasonings to taste with salt and pepper. Cover and store in the refrigerator until ready to use.

Fresh Herb Vinaigrette

This herb vinaigrette can be used as a fragrant refreshing salad dressing or as a marinade for chicken cutlets or pork chops. It will keep refrigerated for up to 2 weeks.

MAKES 1 CUP

¼ cup rice wine vinegar
2 tablespoons balsamic vinegar
2 tablespoons lemon juice
1 small shallot, chopped
2 tablespoons thyme leaves
2 tablespoons oregano leaves

1 tablespoon tarragon leaves
1 tablespoon Dijon mustard
Salt and freshly ground pepper to taste
¾ cup olive oil

Place the vinegars, lemon juice, shallot, herbs, mustard, salt and pepper in the bowl of a small food processor or blender. Process briefly to combine.

With the blender running, slowly add the oil in a steady stream. Continue blending until the mixture is creamy. Adjust seasoning with salt and pepper. Transfer the vinaigrette to a jar, cover and refrigerate until ready to use.

Blue Cheese Dressing

This dressing is delicious as a dip for crudités or grilled chicken fingers as well as spooned over sturdy greens such as romaine lettuce or iceberg. It will keep refrigerated for up to 2 weeks.

MAKES ABOUT 2 CUPS

1 cup mayonnaise
¾ cup blue cheese, crumbled
½ cup sour cream
¼ cup buttermilk

1 tablespoon white distilled vinegar
2 tablespoons lemon juice, or to taste
Tabasco to taste, optional
Salt to taste

Place the mayonnaise, ½ cup cheese, sour cream, buttermilk, vinegar and lemon juice in a mixing bowl. Whisk until well blended and smooth.

Stir in the remaining cheese and season to taste with the Tabasco and salt. If the consistency is too thick, thin the dressing with some buttermilk. Refrigerate until ready to serve.

Compound Butters

Compound butters are the traveling chefs' best friends. Easy to make, they can be stored in the freezer, ready for service at a moment's notice. Use them as an instant seasoning or basting ingredient on poultry, meat, fish or vegetables—a little goes a long way.

Roquefort Butter

This butter is the classic for red meats. Place a small disk on top of each serving of steak or lamb while they are resting after grilling; the butter will melt on contact with the hot meat, producing a quick unctuous sauce. Or check out the Steak with Roquefort and Walnut Sauce (on page 64).

MAKES ABOUT 1 CUP

1 medium shallot, finely minced
½ cup dry white wine
4 oz Roquefort cheese or non-creamy blue cheese such as Stilton, room temperature

8 tablespoons butter, room temperature
Salt and freshly ground pepper to taste

Combine the shallot and wine in a small saucepan. Bring to a boil over medium heat and reduce until the liquid is almost gone. Remove from the heat and cool.

Cut the Roquefort and butter into ½-inch cubes and place in the bowl of a food processor. Add the shallot mixture, salt and pepper. Process until well blended. Do not over process or the mixture will become oily. Roll the mixture into a log and wrap in plastic wrap. Refrigerate until ready to use or freeze.

Anchovy Butter

Anchovy butter is a natural with seafood, either grilled or poached. For some intriguing pairings, use it as a basting ingredient on grilled lamb or tossed with steamed vegetables.

MAKES ABOUT 1 CUP

6 anchovy filets, rinsed and crushed
2 tablespoons balsamic vinegar
Juice of ½ lemon
½ teaspoon thyme leaves, minced

4 to 5 basil leaves, minced
8 tablespoons butter, softened
Freshly ground black pepper to taste

Place all the ingredients in the bowl of a food processor except the butter and process until finely chopped. Add the butter and some ground pepper and blend until smooth.

Do not over process or the mixture will become oily. Roll the mixture into a log and wrap in plastic wrap. Refrigerate until ready to use or freeze.

Ancho-Lime Butter

Spread this Mexican-inspired butter on grilled vegetables, including corn, either grilled or steamed.

MAKES ABOUT 1 CUP

1 dried ancho chile, seeded
3 tablespoons chopped fresh coriander
1 tablespoon fresh lime juice

½ teaspoon ground coriander
½ teaspoon chili powder
8 tablespoons butter, softened

Soak the ancho chile in warm water for about 30 minutes until softened. Drain and dry on paper towels.

Place all the ingredients in the bowl of a food processor except the butter, and process until finely chopped. Add the butter and blend until smooth. Do not over process or the mixture will become oily. Roll the mixture into a log and wrap in plastic wrap. Refrigerate until ready to use or freeze.

Orange-Rosemary Butter

This fruity combination is a definite winner on steak and lamb. For a fragrant roast chicken, tuck some softened butter underneath the skin before putting in the oven.

MAKES ABOUT 1 CUP

2 shallots, chopped
1 garlic clove, chopped
2 tablespoons minced fresh rosemary
1 teaspoon grated orange rind

1 tablespoon freshly squeezed orange juice
8 tablespoons butter, room temperature

Place all the ingredients in the bowl of a food processor except the butter and process until finely chopped. Add the butter and some ground pepper, and blend until smooth. Do not over process or the mixture will become oily. Roll the mixture into a log and wrap in plastic wrap. Refrigerate until ready to use or freeze.

All-Around Barbecue Sauce

You could buy commercial BBQ sauce, but why should you? This recipe works well as a basting sauce for meaty fish such as salmon and of course, any type of meat. The sauce will keep for up to 3 weeks tightly covered and refrigerated.

MAKES 1½ CUPS

3 tablespoons vegetable oil
3 garlic cloves, minced
1 small onion, minced
1 cup ketchup
½ cup dark brown sugar
¼ cup Dijon mustard

2 tablespoons Worcestershire sauce
Juice of 1 lemon
2 teaspoons Tabasco sauce or to taste
2 teaspoons chili powder
1 teaspoon celery seeds

Heat the oil in a large saucepan over medium-high heat. Add the garlic and onion and sauté until soft and lightly golden.

Add the remaining ingredients and bring to a simmer, stirring constantly. Reduce the heat to medium-low and cook for 20 minutes, stirring once in a while.

Remove from the heat and cool. Cover and refrigerate until ready to use.

Minutemeals.com Chefs

Speeding

The chefs at minutemeals.com know all about the art of preparing delicious and nutritious meals in 20 minutes or less every night of the week whether you are coming home from work or on a relaxing vacation. Working together, they have assembled a series of recipes that offer complete menus from soup to nuts, time saving strategies, shopping lists and useful tips, all presented in an easy-to-follow game plan.

Flavors

Between them, this gifted group of culinary professionals has years of experience in the kitchen and put that experience to work for you by using every trick they know. Each chef comes from a different culinary background and style, giving the recipes their unique, diverse flair. The result? Good, homemade meals in a fraction of the time. Want a Tunisian-inspired meal, chili from scratch or some great American fare? It's all there for the making in just 20 minutes.

Their contribution to *Cooking on the Road with Celebrity Chefs* includes straightforward yet inviting recipes using easy to find ingredients.

For Great Ideas on Tasty Speedy Meals:

www.minutemeals.com

Minutemeals: 20 Minute Gourmet Meals (John Wiley & Sons, 2002).

Minutemeals: 3 Ways To Dinner: New Ideas for Favorite Main Dish Ingredients (John Wiley & Sons, 2002).

Minutemeals: Vegetarian: 20-Minute Gourmet Menus (John Wiley & Sons, 2002).

Minutemeals: Quick and Healthy Menus (John Wiley & Sons, 2003).

Minutemeals: 5-Ingredient Main Dishes (John Wiley & Sons, 2003).

Frank Ottomanelli

When the Ottomanelli brothers settled in New York in 1932, they brought with them a 200-year tradition of Bari, Southern Italy. When they opened their first butcher shop in Manhattan's West Village, they created their own tradition: providing the best quality meats available, elevating standards in their craft and extending courteous, knowledgeable service to their customers. Quickly, the name Ottomanelli became synonymous with excellence. Today, in this era of anonymous supermarket chains, they still provide an old-world craftiness and an unparalleled care and integrity for their products—qualities that earned them a loyal following of discriminating patrons expanding well beyond New York City's borders.

A few years ago, Frank Ottomanelli brought the family brand and its superlative quality to new neighborhoods using modern day convenience and innovative technology. At OTTOMANELLI.COM, customers will find top of the line prime aged meats, specialty meats and poultry, a wide assortment of prepared meals from F. Ottomanelli kitchens and pasta, sauces, seafood, breads and desserts personally outsourced by Frank. An intimate dinner for two or a grand gathering "Ottomanelli-style" are now available overnight, all over the country, with just a click of a mouse!

Today, Frank is again opening new frontiers with his new venture, CAMPOTTO.COM, offering restaurant quality meats and products delivered right to your RV doorstep. The line includes assorted cuts of beef, chicken breasts, lamb and more. Each serving is flash-frozen, individually packaged for convenience and minimal waste, and ready to grill. The new line is available in select campgrounds around the country—make sure to inquire when making your reservation. Or stock up before you go by visiting:

www.campotto.com
www.ottomanelli.com

Resources

Kalustyan's

123 Lexington Avenue
New York, NY 10016
212-685-3451
WWW.KALUSTYANS.COM

A large selection of Indian and Asian spices, herbs and dried chile peppers. You may want to browse through their interesting collection of condiments and salsas.

La Tienda

3601 La Grange Parkway
Toano, VA 23168
888-472-1022
WWW.TIENDA.COM

Imported foods from Spain, ranging from chorizo and Piquillo peppers to olive oil and Manchego cheese. They also carry interesting kitchen tools and tableware. If you are staying around Williamsburg, VA, you may want to visit their retail showroom.

Murray's Cheese

254 Bleecker Street
New York, NY 10014
888-MY-CHEEZ (692-4339)
WWW.MURRAYSCHEESE.COM

Offers an extensive, worldwide selection of cheeses. The site is also full of information for storing, serving and all you want to know about cheeses.

D'Artagnan

280 Wilson Avenue
Newark, NJ 07105
800-327-8246
WWW.DARTAGNAN.COM

The leading purveyors of organic poultry, game and specialty meats for restaurateurs, chefs and top retailers around the country. It is also a great source for chorizo, andouille sausages, pates, truffle butter and smoked delicacies, among others.

F. Ottomanelli

61-05 Woodside Avenue
Woodside, NY 11377
800-370-6073
WWW.OTTOMANELLI.COM
WWW.CAMPOTTO.COM

Superior quality meats, sausages, lobsters and prepared foods available from one of the premier butcher shops in New York City. In addition, Campotto.com offers a line of products designed for gourmets on the go.

Photo Credits

title page, *left*, © John Sigler
   center, dinette set in Fleetwood's Providence RV, photo courtesy Fleetwood RV, www.fleetwoodrv.com
   right, Country Coach's Intrigue 530 RV, photo courtesy Country Coach, www.countrycoach.com

page 4, *left*, galley of Country Coach's Affinity Custom RV, photo courtesy Country Coach, www.countrycoach.com
   right, Winnebago's Adventurer, photo courtesy of Winnebago, www.winnebagoind.com

page 5, *left*, © Roberto Adrian
   right, © Jim Jurica

page 6, *left*, © Rasmus Rasmussen

page 8, *left*, © Sandra O'Claire
   right, © Diane Diederich

page 19, *left*, © Wael Hamdan
   right, © Daniel Gilbey

page 21, © Elena Korenbaum

page 22, *left*, © Stuart Pitkin
   right, © Wojciech Krusinski

page 28, Peter Riskind

page 37, *left*, © Sean Locke
   right, © Rick Jones

page 41, *left*, © Janeen Wassink
   right, © Nathan Chor

page 46, *left*, © Ranilo
   right, © Andrija Kovac

page 56, *left*, © Daniel Gilbey
   right, © Greg Nicholas

page 63, *left*, © Greg Nicholas
   right, © Massimiliano Fabrizi

page 75, *left*, © Alex Brosa
   right, © Diane Diederich

page 76, *left*, © Kristi Petzel
   right, © eyecrave LLC

page 93, *left*, © Roberto Adrian
   right, © Ben Phillips

page 103, *left*, © Joseph Hoyle
   right, © Byron Carlson

page 114, *left*, © Daniel Gilbey
   right, © FhF Greenmedia

page 119, *left*, © Daniel Gilbey
   right, © Roberto Adrian

page 121, *left*, © Rayna Januska
   right, © Donald Gruener

page 127, *left*, © Will Louie
   right, photo courtesy TrailManor, www.trailmanor.com

page 129, *left*, © Tan Wei Ming
   right, © John Shepherd

page 132, Peter Riskind

page 134, *left*, © Jillian Pond
   right, © Erxolam Photography

page 143, © Erxolam Photography

page 147, *left*, © Jim Lopes
   right, © Sean Locke

page 158, *left*, © Bluestocking
   right, © Jeffrey Walbel

page 167, *left*, © Jim Jurica
   right, © Marianne Fitzgerald

page 176, *left*, © Monika Adamczyk
   right, © Stephen Walls

page 177, Peter Riskind

page 184, *left*, © Jillian Pond
   right, © Ewa Brozek

page 187, *left*, © Hal Bergman
   right, © Terry J Alcorn

page 193, *left*, © Jim DeLillo
   right, © Jim Jurica

page 200, sink in Fleetwood RV's Bounder, photo courtesy Fleetwood RV, www.fleetwoodrv.com

page 201, © Jason Smith

Index